D1459861

LIVING OUT
LOUD

LIVING OUT
LOUD

SPORTS, CANCER, AND THE THINGS
WORTH FIGHTING FOR

CRAIG SAGER

WITH CRAIG SAGER II AND BRIAN CURTIS

FLATIRON
BOOKS
NEW YORK

LIVING OUT LOUD. Copyright © 2016 by Craig Sager, Craig Sager II, and Brian Curtis.
Foreword copyright © 2016 by Charles Barkley. All rights reserved. Printed in the
United States of America. For information, address Flatiron Books, 175 Fifth Avenue,
New York, N.Y. 10010.

www.flatironbooks.com

All photographs courtesy of the author unless otherwise noted

Designed by Steven Seighman

The Library of Congress Cataloging-in-Publication Data is available upon request.

ISBN 978-1-250-12562-0 (hardcover)
ISBN 978-1-250-12563-7 (e-book)

33614057755547

Our books may be purchased in bulk for promotional, educational, or business use. Please
contact your local bookseller or the Macmillan Corporate and Premium Sales Department at 1-800-221-7945, extension 5442, or by e-mail at MacmillanSpecialMarkets@
macmillan.com.

First Edition: November 2016

10 9 8 7 6 5 4 3 2 1

To my Stacy and my children Casey, Craig, Krista, Riley, and Ryan. You have supported me, and I will fight to be there as long as I can to support you.

CONTENTS

FOREWORD BY CHARLES BARKLEY

I have traveled the world, meeting thousands of people of all colors, creeds, and nationalities, some basketball fans, some not. I have sat with presidents and with Hall of Famers, played alongside the greatest in the game, and watched the next generation. I thought that I had lived life to the fullest. But then I got to know Craig.

His passion for basketball and for sports in general is unmatched. The guy just loves being at sporting events. Listen, if a guy was his school's mascot, you have to believe he has an undying passion for sports.

It was December 9, 1999, and I was home. After playing eight seasons with the Philadelphia 76ers and four with the Phoenix Suns, I was returning to Philly as a member of the Houston Rockets to play my last game as a professional in the city that adopted me out of college in 1984. I had already announced prior to the season that this would be my last, and the 76ers front office invited my mother and grandmother to be there for my final game, complete with a pregame ceremony and recognition of my time in a Philadelphia uniform. At thirty-six, my physical health was simply not where it used to be, and my contributions on the court with the Rockets were diminishing.

It was late in the first quarter when the Sixers' Tyrone Hill went up for a shot and all three-hundred-plus pounds of me rose off the floor to try to block the shot attempt. I didn't get the ball, came crashing down onto the hard court, and ruptured the tendon in my left knee. This was how my career was going to end—being helped off the court in pain. As I was being wheeled off on a stretcher back to the locker room, a familiar face emerged next to me: Craig Sager.

The first time I met Craig was in the early 1980s, when I was playing basketball at Auburn University and Craig came down with a CNN crew before a big home game against the top-ranked UNLV Runnin' Rebels. CNN, like Craig, was still emerging on the national scene, but hey, it was national. Flash-forward a few years to when I was playing for the 76ers in the National Basketball Association. I honestly cannot recall the first time he interviewed me after a game, but I can tell you how I felt: *I have arrived.* You see, Craig has been such a big part of the NBA that being interviewed by him meant that you were somebody. I remember I had the same feeling when Dick Vitale first interviewed me while I was at Auburn.

So Craig and I had a history when he approached me that night in Philadelphia as I lay writhing in pain. Turner was not broadcasting the game, but Craig was on-site to report on my homecoming.

"How are you feeling, Charles?"

"What do you think you injured?"

"Do you believe you have played your last game?"

The relentless reporter in him came first. Obviously, I couldn't know the answer to most of his questions. I couldn't even speak; I was in so much pain.

But then he shared something with me.

"Here is David Levy's phone number. He runs Turner. He has a job for you."

As it turns out, David had been watching the game, and as soon as he saw me go down with an injury, he called Craig and told him to have me call him.

It was an odd time for Craig to pass along the number, but as fate would have it, it changed my life. I had been in discussions with NBC Sports to join their broadcasting team after the season, but I did call David Levy, and the rest is history. Craig Sager impacted my life. But it would be another fifteen years before he *changed* my life.

In the years since our first meeting, Craig has become much more than a colleague; he's been a friend. A lifetime of memories has been built: the 1992 and 1996 Olympics; a Nike trip to Japan with other NBA stars; a visit to his son Craig's junior high school class (though when he picked me up in his Corvette on that rainy day, he had to put the top down for me to fit); and a threat from his mother. Coral and Al Sager lived in the Atlanta area, near the Turner studios. Craig decided to bring me to their house for a visit one evening and the conversation turned to his colorful wardrobe, which I thought he needed to tone down. His father agreed with me.

"Listen, Charles Barkley, you don't come into my house and talk about my son's clothing," Coral threatened me. I couldn't tell if she was serious or joking.

When our good friend and colleague Ernie Johnson was diagnosed with non-Hodgkin's lymphoma in 2003 before missing work for treatment in 2006, it was a punch in the gut. I'd never had anyone close to me suffer from cancer. Fortunately for E.J., they caught the disease early and he responded well to treatments.

So when I learned in April 2014 that Craig had leukemia, it was yet another gut punch, but until I fully understood the seriousness of his condition, I assumed that he would be right back on the air, just like Ernie. I recall visiting him in the hospital in Atlanta shortly after his diagnosis. I was in scrubs head to toe, mask over my mouth to prevent any small germs from infecting Craig. I didn't know what to expect when I walked in. You never know how someone will react to a terminal illness. But while I was there, Craig cheered *me* up. He made *me* laugh. He made *me* feel like he wasn't even sick.

The positive attitude with which he approached life and his work was still there. Even as his battle has grown tougher over the past two years, Craig has always been on the bright side, never wondering if he won't make it, but rather wondering how fast he can make it back.

Perhaps the best compliment that you can give a person is to tell them that they make you a better one. And that is true of Craig Sager. He motivates and inspires me to be a better man. He fights with grace and courage and humor, and never once have I heard him complain, despite some of the deep valleys he has fallen into. It has changed me in ways I couldn't have imagined. I think I am tough, but I am not Sager Strong. I don't complain as much after a visit with Craig. I marvel at how he can have such an awful disease but act as if every day is the best day of his life.

Craig has a huge advantage in his fight in that Stacy is his wife. I admire how she has been a true caretaker for more than two years while also raising two incredible children. Having a support system is critical for anyone facing adversity, and Craig has the best in Stacy, Riley, Ryan, Kacy, Craig, and Krista. His battle is his family's battle. Going through a battle with cancer is not easy, and perhaps even more difficult when you are a public figure. *How is Craig doing? What is the latest on Craig? I read online today that he is back in the hospital; I am so sorry. When will Craig be back?* Well-intentioned family, friends, and strangers all want answers in the grocery store, at the school drop-off, at a tennis match, in the mall, and even while walking the halls of a hospital.

I have been blessed with a lot of things in my life—family, fame, wealth, and the ability to do what I want when I want. Material things come and go, but true friendship lasts forever. I hope that Craig and I grow old together, and I hope that others will be as inspired by his story as I have been by his life.

C.B.
August 2016

LIVING OUT
LOUD

INTRODUCTION

Good things do come from having cancer. It is a little strange to read that line out loud, but it was actually easy to write, because it's true. At least for me. Since being diagnosed with leukemia in April 2014, my outlook on life has been inversely proportional to the effect my disease has had on my body. I have been able to touch people in ways I never thought possible. I have formed friendships with random strangers around the country who are battling their own enemy. I have savored every ounce of sunshine, of sea breeze, of buffalo shrimp, of private moments with my bride and children. The cancer has reinforced my passion for my life's work and my desire to continue doing it.

Most of all, having cancer has made me more determined than I have ever been. I will beat the odds and I will beat leukemia and I sure as hell won't let it stop me from living my life. I have always been a public figure because of my work in sports television and, yes, because of my fancy jackets. When I was diagnosed two years ago, I made the decision that I was not going to hide from the cancer or attempt to shield others from the news. I have lived my life out loud for decades and I was not going to change now.

I am as sunny in my outlook as my fanciful suits are bright and, as you will read, I have always been optimistic and fearless. But make no mistake: this battle has not been easy, and there have been some very dark days. No one wants to see me complain, see me in my worst moments, so I make sure I summon the strength to be positive when others are around.

When I was first approached about the idea of a book, I hesitated, for though I'm kind of like the Forrest Gump of the sporting world, like Forrest, I never intended to be the face of anything. In fact, I've always liked my role because I could be there without being *the* guy. *Biographies are for heroes and famous people*, I thought. But as strangers approached me on the street for photos, as patients sought counsel in the hallways of MD Anderson Cancer Center in Houston, and as handwritten letters overwhelmed my mailbox daily, I agreed that if telling my story helps just a few folks looking for some meaning in this raw deal we call cancer, it would be worth it. Despite my determination to win the battle, I don't know what is in store for me long-term, but I want people to know that even if they're reading this after I'm gone, I never quit and neither should they.

What follows are the collected moments that have filled the journey of my life and my battle of the past two years, and, most important, reflections that were perhaps compelled by the situation in which I've found myself. I don't have the answers, or a recipe for how to beat cancer or, more simply, how to live your life. All I can do is share my story.

I often think about the famous movie *The Pride of the Yankees*. It has always been one of my go-tos for inspiration. During the final scene, where Gary Cooper delivers Lou Gehrig's famous farewell speech, I always find myself leaning in . . .

People all say that I've had a bad break. But today . . . today, I consider myself the luckiest man on the face of the earth.

The Iron Horse and I have something in common. What we might've imagined a terminal diagnosis would do to our spirits, it summoned quite the opposite: the greatest appreciation for life imaginable.

Outside of the main entrance of MD Anderson Cancer Center sits a nondenominational chapel for families and patients, and resting in front of the chapel is a beautiful sculpture with an engraving of part of a Victor Hugo poem:

Be like the bird who
Halting in his flight
On limb too slight
Feels it give way beneath him
Yet sings
Knowing he hath wings

I am the bird and I will keep singing until I can't sing any longer—and then I will sing some more.

PART I

THE MAKING
OF ME

1

"LET'S PLAY TWO"

I was as nervous as I'd ever been. I've jumped out of airplanes, swum with sharks, climbed the Great Wall of China, run with the bulls in Pamplona, been arrested—a *few* times—and recently been told I have months to live. But as I stood in the dugout waiting to be introduced, I could actually feel my heart beating through my blue dress shirt underneath my all-white linen suit. My fingertips were so clammy, they left sweat marks on the baseballs I used for my warm-up pitches under the stands, and I was rocking back and forth on my feet when Cubs manager Joe Maddon, who was to present me with a personalized Cubbies jersey prior to my pitch, walked up to me and lightened the mood with a little banter. As I looked around at the forty thousand Cubs fans in sold-out Wrigley Field on that June evening in 2016, I realized this baseball team, this place, was the touchstone by which I could measure my whole life.

Almost all of my childhood birthdays were spent here, and in the weeks leading up, classmates would try to curry favor with me—bribing me with baseball cards and their lunch snacks—knowing that an invitation to Wrigley hung in the balance. I always got autographs before games from our Cubs heroes, though my father would make me share my prized signatures with my friends who were a bit more reserved—which angered me. One pregame, I remember getting Ernie Banks, Billy Williams, Tony Taylor, and Don Zimmer autographs on their baseball cards. Dad allowed me to keep Banks and Williams but made me give Taylor and Zimmer to my friends who were in tears at their failure to match my aggressiveness.

My bedroom in Batavia, Illinois, about fifty miles from Wrigley, was awash in Cubs paraphernalia—Cubs sheets, Cubs pillowcase, Cubs backpack. I even drew the Cubs logo on all of my school folders and binders, just in case a classmate was unsure of my loyalties.

In my father's old briefcase, a gold-colored aluminum box with two flaps, I kept my most prized possessions as a child—baseball cards. The Topps sets came out every spring, and Schielke's Grocery on Main Street sold the cards in packages of twenty, along with a piece of pink bubblegum, for just a nickel. My Aunt Lil kept me well stocked with a pack in her weekly grocery shopping. Opening a pack was like Christmas morning. The scent of a pink stick of bubblegum was the aroma of a forthcoming afternoon of blowing bubbles. But more important, it was the concealment of what was stacked below. A Hank Aaron, Mickey Mantle, Willie Mays, or, better yet, a beloved Cub: a George Altman, an Al Spangler, a Bob Will, or—a winning lottery ticket—an Ernie Banks, a Ferguson Jenkins, or a Billy Williams.

I devoured the cards, memorizing and reciting the batting statistics, hometown, and height and weight of each player. I looked for deals with my friends, trying to complete a team set and, of course, was *always* open to a trade that involved a Cubbie.

When we weren't brokering baseball card deals, we were on the sandlot next to Peterson's Foundry, which churned out hot metal every afternoon. The lot was really just dirt with a few patches of dead grass, but it was big enough for us to live out our dreams on. We would play four-on-four games of baseball, with actual bases thirty feet apart and intricate rules for what counted as a double or a triple. We could stay out all day in the summer, just like my Cubbies would.

Once we were eight years old and eligible to play Little League, I was crushed when I was drafted by the Batavia Body Company White Sox and not the Batavia Central Pattern Works Cubs. The Little League field was right by the Fox River, and you could often find me at third base in the springs and summers, where I had more talent fielding ground balls than making contact as a hitter. In fact, taking pitched balls to the head and upper torso seemed to increase my on-base percentage.

In high school, my friends and I took the train from Geneva Station, the depot closest to Batavia, into Chicago for games, my parents even giving me their blessing to play hooky from school once in a while to catch a Cubs matinee—all Cubs home games back then were afternoon games. I nearly always got away with it. Nearly. One time, my high school coach caught me on TV as I was catching a foul ball. (Though now that I think about it, why was Coach Tom McMahon watching the game during school hours?)

My decision to attend Northwestern University in Evanston, near Chicago, instead of accepting an appointment to West Point, was tipped by the fact that I wanted to be able to escape on the "L" train to Wrigley at will. I perfected my plan by choosing morning classes just in case I heard the call of the ivy, which I often did.

At the end of the Cubs' 1972 season, my classmate Dan

DeWitt (whom we called "Dimmer") and I hopped on the train to catch the Cubbies' season finale. We scored tickets on the third-base side, right behind the field tarp just beyond the dugout. I had it in my mind that at some point during the game, I was going to run onto the field, to experience—if only for a fleeting moment—the Wrigley grass under my feet. As soon as the Cubs closed things out in the top of the ninth inning, I blurted out, "Let's go!"

Without waiting to see if Dimmer was on board, I sprinted across the third-base line and onto the infield as bewildered Cubs players stood by, I like to think, amused. I touched second base and then ran toward first, by now being hotly pursued by Chicago police officers. I made it to first base and kept running, not toward home but rather toward the stands. I lunged over the fence on the first-base line as thousands of fans stood and cheered. As I raced up the bleacher steps, I noticed Dimmer right behind me. We ran down the ramp at Sheffield Avenue and Addison Street, with the officers still some thirty yards behind us. I thought we would make it. What I didn't know was that the officers had radioed ahead for security to close down the exit gates, and Dimmer and I were quickly in custody, handcuffed together. They walked us back up the ramp, down the stands, and, unbelievably, across the field toward the holding cells.

"We get to do this twice!" I said to Dimmer with a smile.

What was my obsession with the Chicago Cubs? Was it the white uniforms with thin blue pinstripes that brought me in? Was it the afternoon games at the friendly confines of Wrigley, with the ivy, the smell of beer, and the drama of sport? Or maybe it was the joy of watching grown men play a kids' game with a smile? No, my love affair with the Cubs starts and ends with Ernest "Ernie" Banks.

Banks was a star with the Kansas City Monarchs of the

Negro American League when the Cubs, aided by Negro American League's legend Buck O'Neil, signed Banks to a contract in 1953. The Texas native had already played two seasons with the Monarchs, interrupted by two years of military service during the Korean War. When he arrived in Chicago, Banks was the first black player to wear the blue and white. Once he cracked the starting lineup, he not only became a mainstay but was one of the Cubs' most popular players. I was born in 1951, and in my most formative years, Ernie Banks was everything to me.

When we would go to Wrigley, we would arrive early enough to watch Banks take batting practice, and I would marvel at his quick hands, his constantly moving fingers, his phenomenal balance, the way he loaded up his lower half and used his legs to drive the ball. I would admire his white jersey with blue pinstripes, the classic red-white-and-blue Cubs logo over the heart, the blue bear cub inside the red circle on the left sleeve, and the iconic number 14 on the back, as synonymous with Chicago as Michael Jordan's number 23 would become a generation later.

But I was in awe of something more than his hitting prowess. You see, Ernie Banks loved life, loved his job, saw each and every day as a new opportunity, and it showed in his smile, his laugh, his hustle, his desire. "Let's play two!" was his motto, always wanting more out of every day. And he never complained, even when his team was consistently at the bottom of the standings or when he was in a slump.

A life-size poster of Ernie was taped to my bedroom wall and he was the first thing I saw when I opened my eyes every morning. I never once thought it was odd that a young white boy from the farmlands of Illinois worshipped a black man from Dallas, Texas, even though it was a time when segregation was still prevalent in American life.

The highlight of my youth was, as an eleven-year-old, winning a Cubs-sponsored hitting contest and getting to shake the hand of Mr. Cub himself. The picture of the two of us from that occasion remains one of my most treasured sports relics.

I didn't just want to be Ernie Banks the Chicago Cubs All-Star; I wanted to be Ernie Banks the man, and that meant taking on his optimistic approach to life. I decided as a young boy to emulate my hero and look at each day as a gift.

Ernie was on my mind as I stood in the Cubs' dugout waiting to be introduced to throw the first pitch some forty-four years after I had last touched the hallowed grass of Wrigley, and this time, my senses took in everything—the freshness of the grass, the evening breeze, the smell of hot dogs, the sunset rays enhanced by the lights installed in 1988. I thought about all that has happened in my life since I sprinted onto the field in 1972, especially as it relates to my family, all of whom were standing on the field behind home plate.

There was my bride of fourteen years, Stacy, full of splendor and life and my heaven on earth. Next to her stood my oldest child, Kacy, thirty, an NBA blogger, and her sister, Krista, twenty-four, a Tampa resident and a budding golfer. To Krista's right was my oldest son, Craig, twenty-seven, whom we call "Junior" and who is the reason I am still alive today. And there were my youngest children, Riley, eleven, and Ryan, ten, adorned in Cubs paraphernalia, looking on in amazement. It was incredible to have my entire family with me, in addition to the more than thirty cousins, friends, and classmates who had made their way to Wrigley to celebrate with me. After a difficult two years of battle, it was a celebration in many ways for all of us.

And now, ladies and gentlemen, please welcome NBA reporter and Chicagoland native Craig Sager.

The crowd cheered as Joe Maddon insisted that I remove my suit jacket and pull over my head a Cubs jersey with my name sewn on the back, which I eagerly agreed to do. I began my walk to the pitcher's mound. At another time in my life, I would have sprinted onto the field, full of Banks's "Let's play two!" spirit, but the weakness in my legs and my struggles with my balance kept me to a walk, so I made the most of the moment by waving to the crowd like a politician.

Throwing out the first pitch at a Cubs game was a moment that I had never envisioned, but a moment that I had been preparing for, for four weeks, after I received the invitation. My preparation started with throwing a tennis ball with Ryan on the driveway, as my strength had been zapped by the rounds of chemotherapy. But every day, I focused on getting ready for that first pitch, and by the time I arrived in Chicago on May 31, I was ready.

Some first-pitch honorees elect to throw to home plate from in front of the pitcher's mound to ensure the ball gets there. Me? Sixty feet, six inches was the *only* way to do it. Cubs first baseman Anthony Rizzo, himself a cancer survivor, got down in a catcher's stance, punched his mitt a few times, and gave me the nod. I put my right foot on the rubber on the mound and cocked my right arm back. The crowd seemed to go silent as the ball left my hand . . .

Funny how life comes full circle when you aren't looking. So much of my life has revolved around the world of sports, witnessing some of the greatest moments and players in the game. One of the great things about sports is that there is always tomorrow or next week or even next season. You gotta have hope. And for me, that hope started in a small town called Batavia.

2

NO FEAR

Traffic" in my hometown of Batavia, Illinois, was controlled by one stoplight. There were no hotels or motels, no Mc-Donald's. There was, however, Avenue Chevrolet, Hubbard's Home Furnishings, Schott's News, Schielke's Grocery, and an assortment of other retail choices named after their proprietors. Since the big city of Chicago was only a forty-minute train ride away, we were not all that isolated from the real world, but it sure seemed like it some days. With a population of just 7,600 and a high school of five hundred, we literally all knew one another.

Founded in 1833, Batavia was known as the "Windmill City," because six of the largest American windmill factories used to be located within the town limits. Notorious Chicago gangster Al Capone and his gang had used the area as a quiet getaway from the jurisdiction of ATP agent Eliot Ness, and John Dillinger once lived on Batavia Avenue, across the street from where I would live one day.

I was like most boys in Batavia and probably like millions around America, with a curiosity for the world and a passion for sports. Yet there was one major difference that set me apart from all the others: a genuine fearlessness, or, as some may accuse me of, a reckless approach to life.

From my earliest memories, I cannot recall a time when I was afraid. I was never afraid of falling or breaking a bone or even losing my life; never afraid of bad grades in school or missing the game-winning shot; never afraid of my parents or teachers or the police; never afraid that I might not reach whatever dreams I set. That fearlessness could be confused with confidence or even vanity, I guess, but I simply relished thrills. Anything that got the heart racing and made me feel as if everything was happening in the moment.

That's why one night, when I was the fifth wheel with my buddies John Clark and Tom Cornwell and their girlfriends, I decided to climb out of the passenger window and get on the roof of John's car, lie flat on my stomach, and hold on to the metal rim where it met the windshield as John gunned the car to 50 miles per hour on an empty country road. It's why I would drive my own GTO at speeds in excess of 120 miles per hour on the roads outside of town, never fearful of crashing and certainly not afraid of getting pulled over. It's why, when I was twelve, I convinced my buddies to strip down and run along Route 31, a major thoroughfare, in our birthday suits. It's why I would hide behind curtains on the windowsill during roll call in class, before jumping out to throw a scare into Ms. Burly. It's why I was the guy who, in the middle of the horse races at nearby Aurora Race Track, accepted a dare from my friends to climb to the top of Aurora's water tower next to the track. Not only did I make it to the top, but I stood and watched the next race as hundreds of patrons turned their eyes toward me, instead of the finish line. And it is why in the summer of 1967, I decided to elevate the stakes.

The big news in town that year was that the Batavia Public Library had scored a photocopy machine, something most of us had never seen. We were used to the carbon paper handwritten copies, so the fact that for just one nickel you could make a copy of an image was a big deal.

"I have an idea," I distinctly remember telling my buddy Greg Issel.

I could tell he had apprehensions, but I could be persuasive, so Greg and I walked down to the library and strolled up to the machine. Greg was nervous. "I'm not sure we should . . ."

"It's *perfect*," I interrupted.

I pulled a tattered $1 bill out of my pocket, placing it face-down on the copy machine glass, and dropped a nickel in the machine. A few seconds later, out came a copy of George Washington, serial numbers and all. We could make ninety-five cents' profit on every copy *if* we could use the fake bills at a store! We were not copying the front *and* back of the dollar bill, mind you, and of course the serial number was the same on every copy. Even more than that, our one-sided, single-serial-numbered copies were in black-and-white. Still, I thought our plan could work, and we made a dozen copies. We cut the excess paper off of the copies so the fake dollars were the same size as real dollars.

We left the library and headed right to Wilson Street, the hub of activity in Batavia (which meant not a lot of hub), and devised a plan as we entered Olmstead's. Olmstead's was a typical small-town store that sold everything from stereos to potato chips and even had a laundromat in the back. The plan was simple: I would distract the store manager by pretending to be interested in purchasing a stereo while Greg would feed the fake dollar bills into the laundromat's change machine.

I engaged the manager as well as a fifteen-year-old could—

in retrospect, the scene probably looked like Michael J. Fox trying to buy a keg of beer from the old coot in *Teen Wolf.* (Only I didn't have the ghoulish voice or freaky eye effects.) Greg took one of the fake bills, placed it into the metal slot, and pushed the slot into the machine. When the slot popped back out, there was no bill remaining and four quarters had clinked down. In a matter of minutes, Greg had more than $10 in coins. We made eye contact and then casually walked out of Olmstead's and headed right across the street to the Huddle, a soda shop where most of the Batavia kids hung out. The grins on our faces were as wide as a Cadillac. We were rich, for sure, but in my eyes, the fact that we had pulled it off was more exciting than being in possession of a few bucks.

We stayed at the Huddle for what must have been three hours, horsing around, scarfing down milkshakes and hamburgers, and teasing one another and our larger group of friends. Just as I went to put another french fry in my mouth, in walked what I can only describe as a platoon of Batavia and State Police officers and scowling FBI agents, who must have been brought in by the locals. Within seconds, both Greg and I were asked to stand up.

"Gentlemen, you are accused of counterfeiting fraud," one of the officers said. I couldn't help but flash to images of Capone and Dillinger.

Smartass that I was, I tried to talk our way out of it, proclaiming that we were just messing around, a couple of Batavia kids bored on a summer afternoon, and I promised that we would give the few bucks back.

"This is not a local issue, young man," an FBI agent responded. "This is a *federal* crime."

And with that, Greg and I were put in the back of a patrol car and taken down to the Batavia jail. I will admit, I was a bit concerned about what would happen next, but I figured I would find a way out of it; I always did.

Greg's father showed up at the jail first and launched right into a tirade.

"This has to be Sager's stupid idea," his father blurted out. "Greg has never even *been* to the library."

"Mr. Issel," one of the agents replied, "*your* son's fingerprints are all over the laundromat and the coin machine." He then went on to list the litany of state and federal statutes that we had violated.

Next it was my parents' turn. They talked with the agents and officers for quite a while—so long, in fact, that waiting for it to end felt like its own sentence.

With the agreement of the Olmstead's manager, no charges were brought, and the federal officials agreed to let the locals handle it. Greg and I agreed to create and oversee a bicycle registration program for the city and work every Saturday, as well as wash the Batavia police cars as punishment. And that was after my father tore into me.

All in all, this "federal crime" business, the parental fury, and the punishment levied on Greg and me paled in comparison with feeling, at least for a little while, like a gangster.

So is it fair to say that as a boy in Batavia, I was a pain in the ass to some, a class clown to others, a nuisance to society, and a detriment to those around me in the eyes of some of my friends' parents? I suppose so. But I was always on the go, never wanting to miss a moment in life. To me, the fearlessness, combined with my Ernie Banks optimism, simply made for a kid with a thirst for life.

Fear of failure was nonexistent for me. At the end of a basketball game with my team trailing by one, I *wanted* the ball in my hands for the last shot. Even now, when I am on the golf course and there is a ten-foot putt to win a tournament, I *want* to take the shot. Fear of failure is simply not part of my DNA. I always take the chance. You want to know the worst that could happen? You could forfeit the most memorable moment of your life and you'd never know.

But when I look back over my sixty-five years while fighting to add more, I do sometimes wonder *why* I am so driven, *why* I never have regrets, *why* I never stop to consider the *what-ifs*, *why* I must be on the go, *why* I refuse to lose my battle with leukemia. And the answer, like many answers in life, starts with home.

3

HOME

Coral Sager was my idol. Tall, athletic, good-looking, fun-loving, compassionate, and with an opinion on most things in America, my mother simply drew people to her. Never one to fit nicely into society's norms—a needlepoint that read F—HOUSE WORK prominently hung in our hallway—she was a Barry Goldwater fanatic who drove a gold Cadillac with a blue convertible top, to signify "gold" and "water," with a bumper sticker that read AUH2O, a reference to the chemical makeup of those two substances. She taught me how to play golf, throw a baseball, and shoot hoops and was an undeniable presence at all my games.

Mom also loved to take me shopping, and, unlike many of my friends, I relished the chance to go with her. There is something so refreshing about having so many choices and about picking what *you* want. To this day, I love grocery shopping, shopping malls, and doing errands. I went everywhere with my mother when I was younger, and her words and actions shaped who I am today. Mom was fantastically curious. She noticed things that others didn't and encouraged me to try new things, to take risks, to have confidence. She took flying lessons and earned her pilot's license at the age of forty-five, taking to the skies just one time, above Florida, and then never flying again— she had only wanted to prove to my father that she could do it. And Mom, like Ernie Banks, never complained, never let the little stuff bother her.

When her sagging breasts started to interfere with her golf game, she made a decision. While most women would choose femininity and appearance over a breast reduction, my mom figured her golf swing was more important at that point in her life than her breasts, and she improved her score by having them reduced. She also had surgery to replace her left shoulder and never complained about the pain. And rather than wait for her appointment to finally get her cast removed, she cut it off herself with a kitchen knife. She couldn't wait to get more distance off the tee on her golf swings.

When she faced a challenge, she simply found a way to overcome it. She didn't mope and didn't lament her circumstances. She was positive at dawn and dusk, and it rubbed off on me. My mother suffered a great deal of pain later in her life, after a hysterectomy and the shoulder replacement, as well as complications from a lifetime of smoking, yet she never complained, remaining stoic and stubborn and unconvinced that bad days were ahead.

My father, Al, was unlike my mother in some ways, and I always wondered how they had stayed married for so long. While I could do no wrong in the eyes of my mom, my dad always saw ways I could be better.

Dad was a public relations and advertising man and did some speechwriting for the Republican Party and Richard Nixon. My memories of my father mostly revolve around him working. Up early, gone late, working at the dinner table, traveling, on the telephone, busy. He would work twenty-hour days when he ran his own agency, and never give much thought to missing dinner at home with his family for the fifth night in a row. And, unlike my free-spirited mother, my father focused on risk management and always worried about what *might* happen, stressing situational awareness to me and my older sister, Candy. Yet he also never complained about his workload or finances or even the next-door neighbor. That was the environment that I grew up in: never complain, never explain, just do it.

His work ethic was passed down to me at an early age, as I filled in whenever I could for friends on the local paper route, mowed neighbors' lawns, and worked on local golf courses. I even applied to be a trash collector in Batavia, but my small size at the time (five-four and 120 pounds) disqualified me according to the city. I will admit, I didn't work that hard in school, as the subjects came relatively easy for me. And despite my lack of studying, I still managed to be a member of the National Honor Society, win achievement awards in mathematics, and score very well on the SAT and ACTs, on top of starring as Haemon in the school production of *Antigone*.

When I was growing up, my father would share stories with me of his wartime experiences before I was born, when he was in the Army during World War II, serving as a reporter for *Yank* magazine and as a co-host, with Bert Parks, of *The Army Hour* radio show. He flew around war zones, interviewing everyone from Chiang Kai-shek to American generals. I remember it was the amount of enthusiasm he had when he shared these stories with me that made me want to be a storyteller like my father.

Dad always made sure that my sister and I appreciated the power of words, and was most proud of my ability to write, as he viewed writing as a craft to be honed. He lived to see me report on some historic sports stories, but he was never more proud than when an essay that I had written about patriotism went national.

In 1966, when I was a freshman hoping for straight A's, my English teacher told me that the only way she would bump up my grade to an A in the spring was if I wrote an essay for the American Legion essay contest, a national competition for high school students. I titled my essay "How and Why I Should Show Respect to the American Flag."

They call us "teenagers" and give us more publicity than our soldiers in Viet Nam. Mostly, we're pictured as mobs of half-washed, unkempt, long-haired youth, who sneer and rebel at parents, teachers, the military, government leaders or anybody or anything that might be construed as old-fashioned, cultural or patriotic. We're supposed to prefer security over opportunity, the "Jerk" rather than sports, Castro more than the president, rock n' roll over the "Star Spangled Banner" and some of the old members of our set are internationally portrayed burning draft cards, attacking teachers, raising funds for Communists or showing disrespect for our flag.

While I love pizza, fries, pie, shakes, tight Levis, TV, vacations and bigger allowances and qualify at fourteen as a teenager, I'm probably more like the millions of untypical teenagers that get little publicity and you rarely see on television.

We untypical teenagers are happy we were born in America and not in Havana, Moscow or Peiping. When we hear the "Star Spangled Banner" or look up to Old Glory floating at the top of the pole in the schoolyard, it's not just any ordinary song or bright colored cloth that brings us up tall. It's the history behind that music and that flag that we remember.

We stand erect as we remember: the Declaration of Independence, the Bill of Rights, Valley Forge, Gettysburg, the Battle of the Bulge, Pearl Harbor, Korea, Viet Nam, the Statue of Liberty and a Nation whose most historical moments were made in the interest of freedom and justice for all and not with a desire for world conquest. Sure, we're teenagers but unlike most sensational rat packs in our midst, we're proud to be in the greatest nation on earth. Whenever others spit on our flag or tear down our government we know it's only because they despise the fact that we already have what they really want.

The flag should always remind us that freedom will always be ours if we're half the Americans as those before us who made it possible.

This is what other teenagers call "flag-waving." It's what my group calls patriotism. We're in the majority and that flag is here to stay!

Not only did that essay earn me my A, but I placed first in the writing contest for freshmen and sophomores at Batavia High School and eventually placed third in the district competition. The local paper, the *Aurora Beacon-News*, got wind of the essay and reprinted it, catching the attention of U.S. representative Charlotte T. Reid, who had it included in the *Congressional Record* for June 1, 1966. My dad took a copy of that essay with him everywhere he went and bragged about his son to his clients and coworkers at every opportunity.

Rest assured, I was not perfect. When I was a junior at Batavia High, I entered a speech competition and qualified for the regional competition in the category of "Impromptu Speaking." As the title indicates, competitors pulled a random topic out of a hat and had one minute to collect their thoughts and deliver an eloquent monologue on the topic. When it was my turn, I reached in and pulled out a piece of paper with the word "euthanasia" on it. *I got this one*, I immediately thought. The Vietnam War was going on; young boys and girls in Southeast Asia were dying or had become refugees or prisoners. I launched into a confident and boisterous address on the plight of youth in Asia. As I spoke, I noticed some eye rolls and heard a few snickers in the audience. I made eye contact with my parents. Perhaps my words were so brilliant that the audience knew I was a shoo-in to win.

When my time was over, the judges all gave me 1's on a 1–10 scale. The host informed me that euthanasia was a form of assisted suicide, not a group of kids in Vietnam. My face flushed with blood, and one second felt like an hour. I could tell the room was waiting to see my reaction. My laugh said it all, and the entire room burst into laughter and applause along with me.

My father was full of clichés and words of wisdom, and he never missed a chance to remind Candy and me, "Don't judge a man until you have walked in his moccasins." He lived that creed. Dad did not judge others based on their skin color or religion or even the amount of money they had in the bank. He saw commonalities, not differences. He felt quite comfortable as the only Protestant on the private Marmion School Board and the only white judge at the *Ebony* pageant in Chicago. The lesson of acceptance was also on display every week on a bocce court in our neighborhood.

Bocce was first played in ancient Rome, and some variation of the game remains popular in Europe and in cities around the world with large Italian populations—like Chicago. Two doors down from where we lived in Batavia, our neighbor Severano Pasetti installed a bocce court in his backyard and hosted weekly neighborhood cookouts and bocce tournaments. For whatever reason, my father took an intense liking to the game, and when he wasn't working he made his way to Seve's backyard and eventually traveled to matches with him and a local bocce team consisting of all Italians—except for Dad. When the national bocce team from Italy went on a barnstorming tour of the United States when I was a teen, my father was selected to be on the U.S. team to take on the world champs at a bocce court set up outside a restaurant in downtown Chicago. The crowd was huge, and many Batavians traveled to Chicago to cheer on Dad and Seve—including me. I am not sure that I can remember ever being more proud to be Al Sager's son.

As was evidenced by his star turn with immigrant Italians in bocce and as the only white man on various nonprofit or educational boards, my father taught my sister and me to see people for who they were, not what they were. In fact, two of my teammates and good friends in high school, Mike Brown and Dennis Graves, were both African Americans from the "Eastside" of Batavia who did not have a lot. My father routinely took the three of us out to dinner after games, and one year he paid for Mike and Dennis to attend DePaul University coach Ray Meyer's basketball fundamentals camp with me in Three Lakes, Wisconsin. I will never forget Mike's eyes when we stopped on our way up to the camp and Mom filled up a large cooler with more snacks and drinks than Mike had ever laid eyes on.

Years later, as I came to *truly* understand the enormity of the race issue through the many places I visited and the many people with whom I spoke, I appreciated the great opportunity my upbringing had afforded me—to choose heroes and, more important, friends based on criteria that superseded race. I never thought of Ernie Banks as black, just the greatest there ever was.

Sports have always been ahead of society, and while Dr. King dreamed of a time when his children would be judged not by the color of their skin but by the content of their character, sports have long been there. I was born four years after Jackie Robinson broke baseball's race barrier, and, with Ernie Banks as my idol, I recognized that it was talent, work ethic, and accomplishments that made Hank Aaron the greatest hitter, Jim Brown the most prolific runner, and Bill Russell the most decorated athlete of my generation.

Despite the important lessons I learned from my father, he was not perfect, and at times he could be overly critical of me and my sister. I actually had teachers in high school who had taught my father thirty years earlier, and I was constantly reminded what a perfect student he was. While my number-nine class ranking in my senior class of 196 was a source of pride for my mom, my dad looked at it as an inquiry as to who the eight ahead of me were.

And during a rare Little League game that my father was actually in attendance for when I was nine, I struck out three times. On the way home in the car, he told me that I had embarrassed him in front of friends and neighbors by playing so poorly, or "sucking," as he put it. No one felt worse about my performance than me, and with the attitude that the more I practiced, the better I would get, I made the decision right then and there on the short car ride home that I would get better. As soon as we got home, I grabbed my baseball glove and went to our backyard and started to throw a baseball against a brick wall, diving after the ricochet—at great risk to my body—to work on my fielding. As tears poured down my cheeks during ninety minutes of practice, my mother came outside and asked me what I was doing. Her warm hug made things better.

As is the case with me, my father's work was his life, and after selling his advertising agency and moving to Florida, he didn't respond well to retirement. Outside of solving the *New*

York Times crossword puzzle and getting beat by Mom at golf, he didn't have many hobbies, so when I had a major assignment overseas, like the Goodwill Games in 1986 in Russia, I started bringing my father along, thinking he might enjoy the atmosphere. As it turned out, his helping me research and write proved to be a rewarding experience for the both of us. I didn't intend to put him back in his element—I just wanted to give him something to do—but seeing my dad's enthusiasm made me realize that his work ethic, the thing I most admired about him, was born from something very positive.

In 1998, Ted Turner asked me to travel to Cuba to help strengthen relations with the Cuban national baseball team so Ted could get a game scheduled between his Atlanta Braves and the 1996 gold medal winners. I took my father along, and we were afforded unique access to a place where time stands still. My father soaked up everything about the culture, civilization, and uniqueness of the Cuban people by asking questions and taking notes, and I was able to see what my father, the former WWII correspondent, had been like as a younger man. Few sons get the opportunity to see their fathers in a younger form, yet after a week in Cuba, I was left with a vivid image that was neither perception nor fantasy but a realization of how I had grown up to be like Dad.

As for the fourth member of our family, Candy, four years my senior, I was always a pain to her. Not only was I the annoying little brother who spied on her dates, but I was the golden child who could do no wrong in the eyes of our parents. When I threw a rock through our front window in an attempt to get my mother's attention so she could escort me across busy Batavia Avenue back to our house, per her edict, Mom, rather than punish me, apologized profusely for not hearing me calling in the first place. Candy was a rebel. While I broke the rules at times, I also would make sure to be home thirty minutes before curfew, but Candy? She would straggle in an hour late. She and I often fought, as many siblings do, and in fact, on one occasion, Mom threatened to drive the car into a tree if we didn't stop fighting in the backseat—and she did just that! I was in fourth grade when Mom drove the 1958 Buick into an elm tree on Batavia Avenue, its 1950s-style heavy chrome-plated steel bumper suffering minimal damage but shredding the bark on the elm, which stood as testimony to Coral Sager keeping her promises. There was also one time when Candy was babysitting me and was so annoyed with my antics that she and a friend tied me to a tree and simply took off.

My relationship with Candy changed after she left high school, got married young, and had two little girls. Her second child, Christy, was diagnosed with PKU, a dangerous and sometimes fatal disease, and was hospitalized for many weeks. The situation was touch-and-go, and every day I went with Candy to the hospital to try to keep Christy's spirits up. I think my sister appreciated my concern and started to see me as a peer, rather than a bratty little brother. Fortunately, Christy survived the early years and grew into a remarkable young woman.

Looking back, growing up influenced by my colorful family, the puzzle comes together for me. Fearlessness was a gift from God. Optimism was a gift from Ernie Banks. Curiosity and strength from my mother. Work ethic and reaching for the stars from my father. That pretty much sums me up.

4

ONE MINUTE

Perhaps the biggest thing ever to happen in Batavia occurred way back in 1912, when the Batavia High School boys' basketball team won the Illinois state title, during a time when all schools, public and private, played in the same division. They still talked about the '12 squad when I was shooting baskets at the metal rim attached to a fan-shaped wood backboard in my driveway in the 1950s and '60s. Through generations, Batavia has been known as the "Valley of Roundball," the city buzzing on game days and quite literally shutting down on game nights as young and old pack Batavia High's gymnasium.

In high school, I realized that baseball was too slow for me—there simply wasn't enough action for a hyper kid. Football was fun to play, but the practices stunk, especially in the heat of summer. Catching touchdowns as a wide receiver was fun, but I found absolutely no enjoyment in the hitting, tackling, and scrimmaging in practice. I simply didn't like the physicality of the sport. I played three seasons as a punter and as a fast—

but short—wide receiver who could catch any pass thrown my way.

Basketball, though, was perfect: constant action and movement; you played the game as you were practicing; and the best players rose to the top fairly quickly. It was a meritocracy and I loved it. I was determined to be a local hero. To be one of the guys for whom the whole town shut down. To help the Batavia Bulldogs win a shiny state championship trophy (or at least one less dusty than the 1912 relic). But playing basketball at Batavia wasn't for the faint of heart.

Coach Don VanDersnick was, simply, a tough son of a gun. A former Marine with a buzz cut, a soldier's mouth, and a relentless drive to extract every ounce of talent from his players. Playing basketball for Coach Van remains the most difficult thing that I have ever done—tougher even than battling leukemia.

To be a basketball player at Batavia High meant surrendering control, time, and freedom of thought to Coach Van. He dictated how short our hair needed to be and was known to kick a player off the team if his hair was a few millimeters too long. He made every player wear a crimson-and-gold beanie every time we stepped outside of school. Failure to do so would result in severe discipline. Players were banned from speaking with girls in school so as to not distract from a focus on basketball. He even gave us each a spiral notebook detailing everything that we could and could not eat or drink year-round.

If life was tough off the court as a Batavia basketball player, on the court it was hell. Every morning before school, parents dropped off their sons in the cold darkness, while other boys rode their bikes or walked to the gymnasium for 6:30 a.m. practice. Coach Van would drill us with the fundamentals of the game: dribbling, passing, defense. Over and over again we would run basic drills until he was modestly satisfied. We worked up a good sweat every morning before showering and making it in time for first period.

Lunchtime? That was reserved for free throw shooting. Players scarfed down whatever food Mom packed that day and then lined up at free throw lines around the gym to work on technique and accuracy.

When the afternoon school bell rang, we mentally prepared ourselves for the most difficult part of being a Batavia player. Before each afternoon practice, we would affix five-to-ten-pound weights to our ankles and not take them off until we left the gym. Coach always believed that if we trained and practiced with extra pounds on our legs, we would feel that much more lightning-fast during games. So with weights strapped around our ankles, we climbed a two-inch-thick rope that hung from the roof of the gym. Up and down, up and down. Then we hustled over to a bench—not to sit, but rather to do standing jumps over the bench, again and again. After these "warm-ups," Coach put us through an intense two-hour practice (with no water breaks) before concluding with the "One Minute."

Many of you who played a sport are familiar with variations of "One Minute," more commonly known as "suicides." Starting on one baseline under the basket, we would sprint to the free throw line and then back to the baseline; then to midcourt and back; then to the far free throw line and back; and then finally to the opposite baseline and back. Coach Van gave us sixty seconds to complete the sprints. Any team member finishing over one minute forced the entire team to do another one. Some days, we might run five, six, or even ten One Minutes. Teammates would throw up, hands resting on knees, completely exhausted. Logically, I never understood how, after finishing five seconds over, I could overcome the dehydration, exhaustion, and lactic acidosis and possibly do it even faster. But somehow I dug deep, like Coach Van knew I would, and found a place I never thought existed and completed it in under sixty seconds.

Why did I and so many others sacrifice and endure the torture of Coach Van? Well, for one thing, because the games were so much darn fun. I loved the competition. For another, being a member of the Batavia High School basketball team brought with it a status in school and out.

And if you thought that Coach Van and I and my teammates took basketball seriously, you should have seen Coral Sager.

In a hotly contested game against one of our basketball rivals, East Aurora, she marched onto the court to protest a referee's call and, in not so family-friendly terms, insisted that we were getting hosed. Unable to give a fan a technical foul, the ref weakly defended his position until two policemen came to his rescue and asked my mom to return to the bleachers. When she refused, the men in blue shrugged their shoulders, put her in handcuffs, and led her out of the gym. She exited to a standing ovation.

When I was a high school freshman, I played with senior Dan Issel, who would become an NBA Hall of Famer, and junior Ken Anderson, who would find his calling as an MVP in the National Football League. I was only five feet seven inches tall and wouldn't hit my growth spurt until college, but I played my part as a backup point guard. With two of the tallest parents in town (Mom was six feet even, and Dad was six-three, as was Candy, the second-tallest student at Batavia High, behind the six-nine Issel), I was destined to grow. The coaching staff wanted to redshirt me for a year with a study program in Europe, but I was not the least bit interested and patiently moved up the roster from number 3, reserved for the smallest players, to number 32, for the tallest ones, as my skills and my height increased.

In the late sixties, we won fifty-four consecutive conference games and five straight Little 7 championships, and we were annually the final small school standing in the state tournament. That was the result of Coach Van's demands.

I was never the most talented basketball player, nor the tallest or fastest, but I believed in myself and I believed that positive thinking actually made a difference. The way you think influences the way you feel, and the way you feel determines how you act. It's been my philosophy since high school. Think positive, believe in yourself, and you will see the result. That's why I made it onto the court during games. By believing.

Just think about the simple act of shooting a free throw. Many players think about *not* making free throws. They flood their brains with everything that can go wrong. Coaches overcorrect and add even more stress to the player. Me? I step to the free throw line and just assume I am going to make it. I miss sometimes, of course, but I never miss two in a row. In fact, before basketball games at Batavia, as my teammates and I took our last free throw practice shots before tip-off, all of them walked off to the bench having made their last free throw. I always ended my pregame warm-up after *missing* a free throw, because I had so much confidence that I would never miss two in a row.

Not unexpectedly, I could not appreciate the tactics or approach of Coach Van until I was a grown man. I respected him, but I did not fear him. He had a unique ability to push us further than we ever thought we could go with an inherent belief that you never, ever give up. I have thought of Coach Van a lot over the past two years as I lay in hospital beds, my body worn down from the needles, the tests, the leukemia. Even on the toughest days, when pain radiated from my almost bald head to my black-and-blue toes, I never thought of giving up. This was nothing compared with Coach Van's practices, although the stakes are higher.

Ask any of my friends or family who have known me over the years and they will all tell you that I am the same guy as a sixty-five-year-old as I was as a fifteen-year-old. Same spirit, same drive, same goofiness, same resolve. When the Powerball lottery grows to a decent amount, I always buy a ticket or two, confident that I will win. Of course, I have not won the jackpot, but it does not discourage me from playing again, still confident that *this* time I will hit it big.

That enduring feeling of hope that tomorrow will be my day, that there is nothing stopping me, has never left. Every year since 1981, I have placed a bet on the Chicago Cubs to win the World Series—that's thirty-five years of losing bets. In December 2015, I put down $1,000 for the Cubs to do it *this* year. You gotta think positive.

Fearlessness: check. Optimism: check. Curiosity: check. Work ethic: check. Belief: check. Determination: check. Hope: check. God, Ernie, Mom, Dad, and Coach Van, thank you. I have needed every one of those attributes over the past two years.

5

FAMILY

In the fall of 1980, I was working in Kansas City as a sports television anchor at the local NBC affiliate and hosting pre- and postgame shows for the Kansas City Royals. I was having a blast as a twenty-nine-year-old working the games, making appearances, and dating. It was at a Royals game that I met a nineteen-year-old girl and, perhaps not surprising for a guy who moves quick, we got engaged after just two dates and married just three months later. The marriage didn't work in the long term, but it did produce three amazing children.

By the time my first child, Kacy, was born in 1986, I was working at CNN and at Turner in Atlanta, covering college football, basketball, track and field, and international events, but my mind was never too far from little Kacy. Every moment that I was home, I held her in my arms. A part of me couldn't believe that I was a father; inside my body, I thought and felt like a kid. But I quickly learned that being a father was both difficult and well worth it. When I was home, I would take Kacy with me to work, to the store, and to games just like my mother had done with me. Kacy (I called her "Big Stuff" because I took her everywhere) was my buddy, and I carried her pictures, her drawings, and her notes to me with me everywhere I went.

When she reached school age, I would drive her to school and then carry her into her classroom, tickling her along the way. When her kindergarten teacher suggested that I was not helping her develop independence by walking her into school every day, I responded that the teacher should worry about the parents who *don't* take their kids to school every day. The conversation eventually led to a meeting in the principal's office, after which I received an ambiguous apology from the teacher, including this gem: "You are a wonderful father and an asset to our class." That note is framed in my basement.

Today, my relationship with Kacy mostly revolves around sports and our shared passion for basketball. She has grown into a remarkable woman, who knows more about basketball and the NBA than I do and who regularly wins her fantasy leagues. When I was first diagnosed with leukemia, Kacy was at the hospital challenging doctors and nurses with questions, protective of her dad, and she soon became a leukemia expert, reciting all of my medications and dosages without prompting. Our relationship is complicated but reassuring, and I have never stopped loving my oldest.

Two years after Kacy was born, my first son came into my life. It can't always be easy being Craig Sager's son, especially when you share his name, and certainly when, during your childhood, you often saw your father on a small television screen instead of tucking you in at night. But being my son also came with some spoils.

In 1996, I was covering an international basketball tournament in Italy with former NBA great Danny Ainge, when he mentioned that despite playing professional baseball for a time, he had never attended a World Series game. It just so happened that the Atlanta Braves were hosting the New York Yankees in the Series, and since we were both flying back from Italy into Atlanta, I invited him to stay for a night and attend a game with me. We changed clothes at my house and jogged over to a local soccer field, where Craig, then about seven years old, was playing. His team, even at a young age, was loaded with talent, and Craig was among its stars. It was always such a proud moment when I could take in one of his soccer or baseball games. I just loved watching him out there.

So Danny, whom few folks at the field even recognized, and I stood on the sidelines cheering Craig on. The score went quickly from 5–0 to 10–0, and the parents on the opposing team started to yell at our coaches for running up the score. This goes on for a few minutes while we score a few more goals and the vitriol coming from the other team's parents gets even louder.

"I can't take this anymore," Danny said to me, and he walked right down the sideline to where these angry parents were still shouting.

"Listen, I am here to watch a good soccer game and a good soccer team," he scolded as the game played on. "If your kid is not good enough to play at this level, then play somewhere else." I will never know if Craig was proud or embarrassed of his father's friend, but I'm never going to ask. As for me, that was the Danny Ainge that I knew, and I just looked on with a smile.

Craig has always been an exceptional athlete, much more so than I ever was. He was the rare eight-year-old playing Little League baseball with kids three or four years his senior. Despite his natural athletic gifts, he always worked hard at his endeavors and out-hustled his opponents.

It has been more than five years since my own father passed away, and I think about him often when I think of my oldest son and my relationship with him. I do think that the older Craig has gotten, the more he understands who I am and what I do. We are blood brothers in more ways than one.

Krista came next, in 1991. My youngest—at the time—and I had a routine when she was younger. Every night when I was home, she would take a bath, brush her hair, and brush her teeth, and then we would lie next to each other in her bed to read *Baby Piggy and the Giant Bubble*. It was a tradition that never got old and was our special time each day to read, to laugh, and to talk. She also had a teddy bear that she called Stitches, which I had given to her the day she required stitches on her forehead after knocking into a door. Stiches went with her everywhere, including on a road trip with me to Detroit. When we went to check out of our hotel, Krista realized she did not have Stitches and we panicked. I figured the bear must have gotten rolled up in the sheets and sent to the laundry. The front desk manager, Martha Richards, allowed me and my daughter to go to the basement laundry, where we looked through the piles of sheets until we found Stitches.

Today, Krista is such a positive, optimistic young woman, who has picked up the game of golf like her father and who has such a big heart. I forget sometimes that she is a woman with a career, a steady boyfriend, and an amazing future. I still think of her as my little girl.

During the Olympic qualifying basketball tournament in Puerto Rico in 1999, my three kids came down to visit for a few days and they were fascinated by the lizards and iguanas present seemingly everywhere you went. They were hard to catch, but with my kids looking on—and with my cameraman, Steve Henry, as my accomplice—I snuck up on a little green iguana on a palm tree and grabbed him by the body. We caught a second one and put both into water bottles with holes poked into them for air. The kids named them Rico and Juanita.

As you might imagine, taking animals into the United States was prohibited, so I did my best to conceal the bottles in my carry-on bag. When I opened the bag in the airport to check on them, there was no longer a "them"—just a "him." Juanita had escaped. Miraculously, we somehow got through the airport, and Rico came home with us. We had fun watching him grow. Since iguanas grow based on the size of their habitat, we kept building bigger and bigger cages and watched Rico grow to more than six feet long! As the kids got older, so did Rico, and he eventually moved to my mother's house and somehow made it to ten. To this day, the kids and I still talk about good old Rico.

My work did take me on the road a great deal, and in some years I was on the road more than two hundred nights, which kept me away from my children. The kids grew accustomed to my absence from their activities, school plays, games, and bonding time. But when we were together, it was all about fun. I always tried to make my trips as short as possible. It was not uncommon for me to take the kids to school in the morning, fly to a city for a few nights, then be back a little over forty-eight hours later, eating lunch with them at school, a McDonald's bag in hand.

I recall one time taking Kacy and Craig to twelve different McDonald's so they could collect all the Happy Meal toys (and a few duplicates) from that series in one day. When we returned home, they graded each McDonald's on its food, prizes, and playground, and attached the Polaroid we took at each location to a page in a book.

As my marriage fell apart and the family dynamic changed,

my relationships with my kids became more complicated. It didn't help that I was on the road so much, driven to succeed, to witness every moment that the world of sports had to offer. But I cherished the moments when the four of us could all be together. I remember being so proud as Kacy marched with her bass clarinet in her hands at the 2003 Rose Bowl, with her brother, her sister, and me cheering from the stands.

I may not have always been as attentive a father when the kids were little. I admit that I would often take Craig to an Atlanta-area toy store and have him pick out a new item, which he then would play with on the floor of the nearby Hooters while my buddies Gus Larrison, Crazy Steve Welch, and Hammond Reynolds and I enjoyed some beers. I was one of the founders and owners of the more than one dozen locations of Jocks & Jills, a sports bar in Atlanta, and when Kacy and Craig were toddlers, I was known to put them in the Pop-a-Shot basketball netting so they couldn't crawl far.

Perhaps my parenting skills were a little unconventional, but I loved being a dad. Yet as I turned fifty, something was still missing in my life.

Though my first marriage did not end well, I was not disillusioned by love or even by the idea of marriage itself. In fact, I was driven toward it. I wanted to experience real, passionate, and true love, and I looked forward to finding a life partner. I knew the goal, but getting there would not be easy. Finding a soul mate—and someone who could put up with me, my travel, and my sense of adventure—would not be easy. So I dated a lot, and it wasn't until December of 2000 that the search ended.

A friend kept telling me about this girl, a beautiful blond Midwesterner who had the smarts to match her good looks. My friends had tried to set me up before, but it had never worked out long-term.

"Craig, no—this time I am serious," my friend Larry Young told me. "She is your dream girl." He repeated this last part three times in one conversation. Every time Larry would run into her in Atlanta, he would immediately call me to remind me that my true love was in front of him.

On December 28, 2000, Turner broadcast the MicronPC .com Bowl in south Florida, and I intended to fly directly to San Antonio the next day to meet up with a bunch of college buddies to watch our alma mater, Northwestern, play Nebraska in the Alamo Bowl on the 30th. But after several flights were canceled due to inclement weather over the Gulf of Mexico, I flew to Atlanta, where I planned to stay at the Wyndham Hotel in Midtown. (At this point in my life, I was on the road so much that I saw no need to have a "home" in Atlanta. My parents had moved to the city from Florida in the 1990s, so I kept my wardrobe in their guest room and came by when I needed to refresh the outfits.)

Across from the Wyndham was the original Jocks & Jills restaurant and sports bar. I made a point of stopping in. On this night, after I landed, I remembered that the NHL Atlanta Thrashers were playing at home, so I then went to the Jocks & Jills location in the CNN Center to join the postgame crowd.

Whatever disappointment I felt from the travel inconvenience was immediately forgotten as I walked into Jocks and instantly spotted my dream girl—a down-to-earth goddess, a statuesque blond beauty, just as Larry had described. The image of a striking European model in stark contrast to the jersey-and jean-clad hockey crowd was remarkable. I knew she had to be the one Larry had been telling me about. After a few introductory pleasantries, we talked about her time as a dancer for the Chicago Bulls' Luvabulls, and we connected over a love of basketball and sports. Since she came from a family with four boys, she wasn't afraid to mix it up, either. On top of that, she had a biology pre-med degree from the University of Illinois at Chicago. She was beauty *and* brains.

After some friendly and flirtatious exchanges, I was done. Done.

"I am already falling in love with you," I told Stacy, and I asked her to come with me in the morning to San Antonio for the bowl game, which I still planned to attend.

"No, I just met you!" she protested.

I guess she had a point, considering that the game was the next day.

We went to the original Jocks & Jills, at Tenth Street and Peachtree, for a nightcap, and as she left I kissed her goodbye and literally gave her the shirt off my back. It was a souvenir I had bought after walking over a bridge in Sydney, Australia, a few months prior when I was covering the Olympic Games—a bridge that, ironically, she had walked across a year earlier. In return, she gave me her phone number, which I literally wore out the next day when I finally did arrive in San Antonio. During my trip, Stacy was all I could think about. She was funny, intelligent, caring, and stunning, and she knew how to have a good time.

When I returned to Atlanta on New Year's Day, I had a lunch meeting with my friend and business partner Doc Rivers, and I invited Stacy to join us. Doc was impressed with Stacy's well-informed input on a myriad of subjects, not to mention her gorgeous looks, and gave me a wink of approval, as if to say, "She's a keeper—don't blow it!"

After lunch, Stacy told me that she would be back at Jocks &

Jills in Brookhaven later that evening for a friend's birthday party, and I coyly told her I might be there as well.

That night I would not let her out of my sight, and when the bar closed, I offered to walk her back to her nearby apartment. She invited me in but soon said it was time to go home.

"I don't have a home," I replied, and in the spirit of honesty, it was true. My home was on the road.

"Well, you can't stay here, but you can call me tomorrow," she said.

As I walked aimlessly down Peachtree Street at 2:15 a.m., I realized that the opening was there, and after walking to the Ritz-Carlton in Buckhead to secure a room for the night, I decided I couldn't wait to see her again. The words of the Lila McCann song "I Wanna Fall in Love" were ringing in my head: "I wanna fall in love, I want to feel that rush."

I called her the next morning and asked her out on a date and wouldn't take no for an answer. I put on the full-court press. And we have been together ever since. I am actually closer to her mother's age than hers, and Aaliyah's song "Age Ain't Nothing but a Number," about a young girl falling for an older man, became our anthem.

On one of our early dates, we were sitting on the patio at— where else—Jocks & Jills when I did a typical Sager thing.

"Let's go to Vegas," I said. "Right now."

Stacy looked at me funny, like I was probably joking but she was not sure.

"Let's go," I said. "No bags. Right now."

When she was convinced I was 100 percent serious, she . . . *agreed*.

We took MARTA, Atlanta's public rail system, down to the airport. Before we got on the plane, Stacy had one request.

Although she was twenty-eight, she was still the youngest, and the only girl, among the five Strebel children, and after losing her father at age ten, she and her mom had developed and maintained a trusting and close relationship.

"I would feel a lot better if you would call my mom just to let her know I will be fine."

I agreed, and a minute later I was on the phone with Mary Jo, my future mother-in-law.

"I love your daughter," I confessed. "She's my dream girl, and I want to marry her."

It was all such a blur, I was so excited.

"Promise me two things, Craig," she said to me. "Never lie to her and always treat her right."

We were engaged in June 2002 and married six months later—just eighteen months after we first met—in front of fifty family members and friends at the Atlantis in the Bahamas. Our wedding ceremony took place outside on the resort property, with Christina Aguilera, unexpectedly, performing a concert in the background. The reception took place on a loud and rocking rented boat floating off the island. I toasted my friend Larry Young for making it all happen. And for my good fortune to have Stacy as my bride and to have such good friends, I showed my gratitude and excitement by doing a backflip off the second deck into the water.

Some friends asked me why I wanted to start over at the age of fifty; others wondered why I would give up the single life or want to be a father again at such a ripe age. What they don't understand is that when you meet the right person, you just have the answer right in front of you. I couldn't wait to be a father again.

When Riley was born in 2004, I had no idea what fatherhood

would be like the second time around. I was in my early fifties, but still in good shape, so I wasn't concerned about my ability to keep up with her. I also had the benefit of wisdom.

Riley has become an all-around wonderful young girl. Smart, athletic, kind, and sincere, she continues to blow me away with her success in tennis, in the Science Olympiad, and in her schoolwork. There is nothing that she cannot do. It has been a true blessing to have the chance to watch another child grow up, and just looking into her eyes still melts my heart and pushes me to fight harder against my disease, to make sure I can watch her for years to come. She has maintained straight A's, and at her elementary school graduation she received the Cindy Richards Woody Award for excellence in academics, sports, morals, and citizenship. Among her words in accepting the honor:

> *My father was diagnosed with leukemia two years ago and as a result, my mom had to be his full time caregiver. I was often left to motivate and figure things out on my own, but I never gave up. As an upcoming sixth-grader, I now understand the responsibility and independence as I grow older to make decisions on my own. This is what makes me the person I am today.*

Ryan came next, in 2006, and has a motor that doesn't stop, which both concerns and exhilarates me. It's like looking in a mirror. He is constantly on the go, from one activity to another, never able to sit still and just relax on a couch. I love his curiosity and his love of sports. Like Craig, he is so much better an athlete than I ever was, and perhaps his passion for tennis will take him places to make history, not just witness it. He has shown himself to have the "it" factor for competitive superiority at an early age, with multiple titles playing in an older division.

In 2015, Ryan had a school assignment to write about his hero. I keep this with me everywhere I go:

> *My hero is my Dad. He taught me that it is always important to be generous, to be dedicated, to be brave, and to never give up. My Dad inspired me to never give up. He always told me that if you want to be good at something you must be dedicated. You must go at it and try your hardest. Without my Dad, I would not be a good tennis or basketball player. My Dad got really sick right before my birthday. He was in the hospital while I was having my birthday. But my Dad did not give up. He kept trying to get healthy; he tried to be there for me. He never gave up. He was really brave in the hospital getting all those shots. His one goal was to get back to work and to his family. That is why my Dad is my hero.*

I want Riley and Ryan to live as normal a life as possible, which means I have never wanted them to come to the hospital every day or give up their friends or activities for me. During my long stays in the hospital, Stacy will show me videos of the kids playing sports, and our phone conversations have kept us close. Although my treatment schedule keeps me from coaching Riley and Ryan full-time, I love to watch them compete in both individual and team sports. Riley will contribute any way she can to help her team win, while Ryan, like his idol, Kobe Bryant, prefers to do it all himself.

But even off the fields of competition, Riley has excelled. Last year, she was selected to the WLES (Liberty Elementary School) news team, where she rotated between anchoring the morning announcements, running camera, and operating the teleprompter as the school news was broadcast throughout the school's classrooms. I emphasized to her that she should rehearse her script—and never blame a faulty teleprompter operator for a glitch—and practice the pronunciation of the birthday kids' names for the daily birthday announcements, as it may not seem like a big deal to her but it is to the kids throughout the school. Oh, and smile whenever an appropriate opportunity arises. An anchor with a smiling personality is certainly more appealing to the viewer. It was definitely a valuable experience, and, with a vested interest, I became the proud father of TV Riley and her multitasking television education.

Like Riley, Ryan was also chosen for all of the accelerated academic programs. For the past two years, he has been the recipient of the school's math award. By taking a practical-usage approach to mathematics, we have turned problems into skills: addition and subtraction mastered by differences on the scoreboard; multiplication and division by converting pitchers' ERA and batters' batting averages; and fractions by comparing a player's shot selection with his team's field goal attempts. He may be only ten, but if your local bar needs a square pool for the Super Bowl or your workplace is lacking an office pool for the NCAA Tournament, Ryan is as adept as anyone to run it.

But of all of the special and proud moments that I share with my youngest children, perhaps the best are the times when Riley walks to my closet with me, picking out ties to match my combinations of jackets, shirts, pants, and shoes for me to wear on-air. Even when her selections don't truly match, I wear them anyway, because she is my daughter.

Over the years, I have tried to be a good father, but because of my work, there have been birthdays, soccer games, and breakups that I was not home for. And, yes, I was much more interested in making sure my children had fun than dispensing advice. Being a father is the greatest gift in the world, and the memories of my children are seared into my life's book. Am I a good father? I will leave that to my kids to decide. I know that I do the best that I can. But you know what? Instead of just hearing it from me, why doesn't Craig Junior share his thoughts on growing up a Sager?

6

Growing Up Craig Junior

Sports have been a part of every day of my life. My first
word was "ball." The first day of school was an annual
event that gave me a chance to model my favorite jersey
or team. I learned cities and states by their college and pro
teams. I remembered people by their favorite sport or
team. My math skills were sharpened all year long by the
sports stats my family and I were constantly calculating in
our heads. Sports preserved a window into the past,
challenged my memory, and sparked a curiosity to find the
origin of every story and journey. They also trained me to
watch and listen with the purpose of learning and improving.
The unpredictability of sports taught me how to question,
react to, and forecast the world around me. Sports introduced
me to the full spectrum of emotions and allowed me to see
beyond uniforms and roster numbers.

We lived on a golf course with enough space in the
backyard that Dad installed a concrete track wreathed
with green Astroturf and painted lanes. The island of pine

straw and two tall Georgia pines in the heart of the track framed a row of baby-blue seats from Fulton County Stadium, giving spectators the perfect view of the backyard Olympiads.

Our garages looked like storage closets at a high school gym and were used as soccer goals more than parking spots for the family cars. The roof was a multi-angular backstop for tennis balls and pop-fly drills. The gutters were a mass grave for balls. Only the sunset could intermit the recurring field day.

I spent my childhood going from game to game and practice to practice. Dad taught me that every game was the most important game, and there was always a Sager there to cheer you on. Christmas lists and birthday wishes centered around sports. Trophies, press books, memorabilia, and relics of sports history decorated our house. Our kitchen table was a booth from the sports bar my dad owned. The wallpaper in our basement consisted of panels of baseball cards.

Our family was always in pursuit of fun; sports just happened to be the thing we loved most. Dad was the ringleader of this circus, and he could and would find the fun in anything. Every activity was an adventure, and there was always a reason for celebration. He was a parade everywhere he went, and I was the kid smiling on the float, along for the ride.

Witnessing his need to stay on the go taught me the importance of committing yourself to each moment, even if I was unaware of the lesson as I was learning it. It never occurred to me that other families didn't share this "go big or go home" mentality, and it wasn't until this extreme dedication to the task at hand began to set me apart from my peers that I realized it wasn't the norm.

The first time my Sager work ethic was recognized was when I was handed the Hustle Award after my first season of Little League soccer. I was just trying to win each game and make my playing time count, and I didn't think considerably about the award or the effort I had displayed as I heard my name called in the trophy presentation after the last game. Then my dad marched over, his face beaming, forming the unmistakable sign of victory with fists held high in the air. I asked him what he was so excited about and he told me that the Hustle Award was the most important award that I could receive. His pride at that moment was beyond any reaction to a goal I scored or a game I won. That newly discovered bond between us grew and became the trait I admired most in us and in others, as well as the driving force in my belief that through hard work, I could do literally anything.

There was a specific conversation the two of us had back in 2008 that reminded me of that moment and the impact it had on my life. After a lackluster high school football career, I was determined to prove just how far my work ethic could take me by attempting to walk on as a wide receiver at one of the top football programs in the country. The University of Georgia was fresh off its 41–10 Sugar Bowl victory over Hawaii, and I arrived for day one of winter conditioning to fight for a roster spot on one of the nation's top-ranked teams. After surviving the first days of conditioning, the players were informed that workouts had been moved up to 4:30 a.m. I picked up my phone and called Dad to share my excitement over this added degree of difficulty.

"Everyone is going to have to get up earlier," I said, celebrating. "This is perfect. The harder these workouts are on us, the better chance I'm going to have at making this team. No one is going to outwork me."

As a former walk-on himself, he instantly understood my mind-set and shared my confidence that it would be my attitude that was going to earn me a spot on the team.

Eight months later, he met me on the field of the season opener against Georgia Southern for a quick picture and to tell me how proud he was. My attitude had paid off, and I could feel my family's pride as I hustled out of the tunnel with the number-one team in the nation.

My jubilation was short-lived as the first of my three season-ending surgeries sidelined me. I also began to settle into my major courses in college, and with the family all on our own separate paths, sports were no longer a shared family activity. I had to discover my own perspective and relationship with sports. My journalism classes, not surprisingly, began to challenge my outlook on sports. I studied the politics and laws behind the industry, a much less personal way of looking at it. Classes were so different from what my dad had taught me about sports. I was taught to always consider the player underneath the jersey—that every athlete is a person with a family and aspirations. Suddenly, I was learning to view sports as a business and how to profit from it.

It wasn't until I graduated, recovered physically from the toll of college football, and got my first full-time job in sports, as a writer for Score Atlanta, a sports marketing company in my hometown, that I felt at home again. I went to fifty-five football games during my first season on the job, and I worked around the clock and lived and breathed sports every day. I loved knowing that while I was in a press box and going into locker rooms, my dad was doing the same thing somewhere else, just on a different and more flamboyant scale. He had covered high school games early in his career as well. I felt connected to him through sports, even though we saw each other less often and less often with our overlapping schedules.

Distance never mattered, and through my actions I was connected to him. My work ethic, determination, and positivity all came from my dad and are part of who I am. I always admired him for his passion for his work, as I knew just how much it meant to him. And it's something I want to replicate myself. His work is who he is. And that's why the news in April 2014 was devastating for everyone.

PART II

THE FIGHT BEGINS

7

GREEN ALE

Running has been part of my daily routine since I was twenty-four years old. The now pastime started on my birthday that year, when I ran one lap around a track in Florida for each year of my life, raising money for charity, through the generosity of my friends and family. Decades later, I was still running: every day, every city. I felt alive working up a deep sweat, getting the blood flowing, and taking in the sights and sounds of whatever environment I found myself in: along the Embarcadero of San Francisco and the historic waterfronts of Boston, feeling the winds off of Lake Michigan and the sand beneath my feet on the beaches of Los Angeles. I rarely kept track of time or distance; I just ran, the occasional thought crossing my mind, but mostly enjoying the rare opportunity to explore one of the many incredible cities and towns to which my job took me. Running is a way to sneak a tiny vacation into a business trip.

That's exactly what I was doing on a beautiful April morning in Miami in 2014, when I was in town to cover a Miami Heat basketball game for Turner Broadcasting. With lightweight shoes on my feet, I left the Four Seasons Hotel and headed south toward the Key Biscayne bridge. I felt the sun beating on my face, heard the sounds of Cuban music emanating from the small stores as I jogged by, and was invigorated by the freedom I was feeling relative to those poor folks stuck behind the wheels of cars jammed on the roads. I crossed the bridge and ran through Biscayne to the old pier, then turned around and ran back to the hotel to get ready for the game.

That night after the game on TNT, I followed my typical postgame routine, which included downing Bud Lights with Victor Victoria and other members of the Turner crew at the Hooters Bayside, one of the more than 250 Hooters locations I have visited during my years on the road. I like the buffalo shrimp.

At closing time, I made my way back to the hotel and tried to get a few hours of sleep before a very early morning flight to Indiana. When I woke up, I was a bit more tired than usual and my feet ached—I assumed from my run. I flew from Miami to Indianapolis and drove to Terre Haute, to speak at a fund-raiser to save the Anderson High School Wigwam gymnasium. As an Illinois native who played basketball throughout his youth, I understood the significance of a small-town high school gym to a Midwestern community, so I was happy to oblige when a group led by longtime friend Terry Thimlar approached me about being part of their effort. I had a game in Dallas the following day, April 10, so after I delivered my speech and chatted with students, parents, teachers, and school administrators, I caught the last flight to Dallas out of Indy.

After the plane landed at Dallas/Fort Worth International Airport and the FASTEN SEAT BELT sign was turned off, I popped up out of my seat, stretched big, opened up the overhead compartment, and grabbed my bag.

Man, that's heavy, I thought.

As I followed my fellow passengers off the plane into the jetway, I slowed down. I changed shoulders carrying my garment bag, feeling a little off-balance. Air travel can of course throw you for a loop, but there was what I can only describe as an unusual disconnect between my brain and my body, and it wasn't just fatigue. As I started to walk again up the jetway, I had to stop some ten steps later and rest my right hand on the metal handrail to catch my breath.

What the hell is going on?

I slowed my breathing, calmed my mind, and, step by step, willed my way through the airport to the waiting car, deciding my lethargy was the result of a particularly busy schedule.

All I need is a good night's sleep, I thought.

Typically, when I arrive in a city, even late at night, I go to the nearest bar or restaurant and grab a drink and a late dinner, often interacting with the other patrons, teasing out stories and sharing a few of my own. But my goal that evening was to check in to the Hotel Crescent Court, brush my teeth, and go straight to bed. As I set my alarm and lay down, I gave some final thought to my strange condition. A thought crossed my mind: the leftover St. Patrick's Day beer that had made me sick in San Antonio a few weeks earlier was clearly not out of my system.

That must be it, I thought to myself. *Green beer.* And I promptly fell fast asleep.

In Dallas, my go-to running path was the Katy Trail, a three-and-a-half-mile-long running-and-biking trail set along an old Union Pacific Railroad line through the heart of Dallas. I typically started at the entrance to the trail, near American Airlines Arena, and just ran, taking in the views of the city and the parkland and observing my fellow trail-goers. It was always one of my favorite runs. But when I woke up on the morning of the 10th, I just had no interest and no urge to run. Apathy was an unfamiliar feeling to me. I called Stacy and shared with her my sudden fatigue from the previous night, and she suggested that I take an aspirin and lie down.

"But I have a huge day ahead of me," I said, "a morning production meeting, a full schedule of player and coach interviews, the game—"

"Well, do you have time before the game?" she asked.

"I guess."

"Then take a nap."

I hadn't taken a nap in years, and I wasn't even sure that I could slow my brain down enough to let midday sleep set in, but after our meeting and interviews, I could barely hold my head up, so I retreated to the hotel, took an aspirin, set the clock alarm, and passed out.

When I awoke, I felt surprisingly refreshed. I smiled at the thought that, once again, Stacy had the answer for everything. I hopped out of bed, threw on my usual rainbow-colored ensemble, and headed to the arena.

The Dallas–San Antonio rivalry was a good one, with All-Star players like Tim Duncan, Tony Parker, and Dirk Nowitzki facing off against one another. Of course, there was also Spurs coach Gregg Popovich, one of the best on the sidelines today and with a strong case for being among basketball's all-time greats. His knowledge of the game, his uncanny ability to make in-game adjustments, and his relationships with his players have produced perennial winners.

During the Mavs–Spurs game that night, I was on point—flowing from one end of the court to the other, listening in on time-out huddles, reporting on injuries, and finding time at short breaks to jot down and edit what I felt were solid postgame questions for Popovich. As soon as the game was over, I walked over to the Spurs' locker room for some quick postgame interviews before heading down the hallway to the Mavericks' locker room. Then, *boom*—the same feeling of weakness and dizziness that I had felt walking off the plane the night before hit me like a charge from LeBron.

Dallas's team physician, Dr. Tarek Souryal, who had operated on my knee a few years back after a skiing accident, caught me leaning against the wall.

"Sager," he said, putting a hand on my back and craning his head to get a closer look at me, "you feel okay?"

"Not really," I said, too fatigued to mount any objection. "Something . . . something is . . . out of whack."

Dr. Souryal looked into my eyes like he was performing an examination. "You need to get to a hospital," he insisted, "right now."

"Can't," I said, shaking my head—an act that itself felt like it took a ton of energy—"I have to do some more interviews."

"*Now*," he said, and with that, he pointed me to the exit to grab a taxi while he called ahead to the hospital before finishing his postgame duties with the Mavericks.

So I wandered onto the street outside the arena and hailed a passing cab, telling the driver to take me to Texas Health Presbyterian Hospital. I was a little scared and, certainly, alone.

8

A MISTAKE

Hospitals have always been depressing places for me. I remember visiting my parents as they neared death, and how, despite wanting to spend time with them bedside, the gloom of the hospital wards wore me down. To see my father, who'd constantly been on the move, confined to the dimensions of a bed far too short for his six-foot-three-inch frame, tubes running from his chest wall and lungs all the way to the ground, a creaky apparatus receiving his diseased blood pus and other lung fluid, was just too much. And my mother, dynamic and vigorous her entire life, was unable to stand on two purple-and-green legs, withered by poor circulation, infected with gangrene, a flesh-eating bacteria that broke down her tissues one by one, leading to this unwanted guest breaking into her bloodstream, with amputation her only chance of survival. Even when I was in the hospital for knee surgery for twenty-four hours, I wanted to break out. I have never been sick. Never missed a day of school or work. (Unless it was for the Cubs.)

The emergency room doctor at Presbyterian Hospital ordered a panel of blood tests as nurses hooked me up to an IV to pump fluids into my body almost immediately upon my arrival. While I waited for the lab results, I began feeling better, even to the point that I was ready to get up and walk out.

When I get out of here, I thought, *I'm going straight to the bar at Hotel ZaZa.*

But I waited for close to an hour, during which I became antsy. It didn't seem a particularly busy night for the ER, so either the doctor was grabbing an extra cup of coffee or the diagnosis was something more involved than leftover green beer.

"Mr. Sager," the doctor said ominously as he walked back through the curtain, "you have been basically walking dead." He went on to tell me that the hemoglobin level in my blood was 4.6 grams per deciliter—and the normal range for a man my age was 14 to 18. Though I had no clue what hemoglobin was, his candid diagnosis told me this was a bad number for an important statistic.

In layman's terms, my body had stopped making new, healthy blood, something that likely had been building for months. The potential causes ranged from a typical virus to internal bleeding to "something more sinister." Doctors began a blood transfusion—one of six that I would receive over the next twenty-four hours—and I was admitted to the hospital for further testing, including a colonoscopy and an endoscopy.

As I was being examined, I wanted to jokingly ask, "Do I have time to run to the ZaZa for a quick beer?" but the doctor's mood was somber and the expression on his face told me I'd better not. I called Stacy around midnight and filled her in on the current situation. She made flight plans to come to Dallas the next day. I felt so alone in that cold hospital room, more alone than I have ever felt, and I was confused about what was going on around me.

After I managed a few hours of sleep, I woke up to find that I was still getting blood transfusions, with needles and tubes protruding from my body. Every few hours, another nurse or doctor would visit me, give me one test's results, and then order another, all of which were inconclusive. I was growing more frustrated by the hour; I didn't understand why the doctors couldn't just figure out what was wrong with me and give me medicine to fix it. Stacy arrived Friday afternoon. With her biology pre-med degree and her experience as a sales representative for pacemakers and defibrillators, she got right to work as my representative, peppering the doctors and nurses with questions. *Have you run a full CBC? Who is the chief resident? Have you put him on antibiotics? What are our other options?*

Saturday morning was more of the same—more tests, no answers.

"No more tests," I finally instructed the doctors. "I'm going back to Atlanta."

"Mr. Sager," one of the doctors cautioned, "your blood levels are still very low. You really need to stay stabilized here. It would not be safe to travel."

Stacy initially resisted also, but seeing how much I really just wanted to go home, she relented. The doctor had no choice and he, too, gave in, but not without travel warnings and instructions to immediately go to an Atlanta hospital upon arrival.

It took some hours to be formally discharged, but finally a kind nurse came in and wheeled me to the exit. I waited by the automatic sliding doors in the wheelchair, staring out at the parking lot as Stacy received the discharge papers at the front desk. She rejoined me and we both stood up and walked outside, where a cab met us at the curb.

"Please take us to Love Field," I said as we climbed in the back. We strapped ourselves in, and Stacy read the doctor's notes as the driver pulled out of the parking lot. She did not share with me the note that read *Could be leukemia*.

When I was young, my father and I shared a fascination with airplanes. On some Saturdays, we would drive the thirty or so miles from Batavia to Mannheim Road, next to Chicago's O'Hare Airport, and park the car and just watch. For hours at a time, we watched the planes take off and land at O'Hare. I was curious as to where the planes were headed, who was on board, and I was awed by the miracle of flight. My father, who had flown often during World War II, loved being in the air and would regale me with stories of harrowing adventures in the skies over Europe and Asia.

Yet on this night in Dallas, the thrill of flying was, of course, subdued. I had to be wheeled through an airport that I have literally run through before—for what I kept telling myself was probably just a bad virus. It was embarrassing.

I could feel Stacy watching me like a hawk, but the short flight was uneventful, and once we arrived back in Atlanta I pleaded with her to drive me home. I just wanted to be in my own bed. She initially objected, but I promised her we would go to the hospital in the morning and she reluctantly steered the car to our home in Canton, about thirty miles north of Atlanta, around 2:00 a.m. I could barely make the walk from the car into the house, and there was certainly no way I could climb the flight of stairs to our bedroom, so Stacy grabbed me by the arm and led me to our downstairs guest room, where I lay on top of the comforter. I had never felt so tired in my life. Despite the past forty-eight hours in the hospital, I continued to believe that all I needed was a good night's rest in the comfort of my own home and all would be fine.

As soon as I closed my eyes, I felt the room spinning. I could feel the sweat and I could hear my heartbeat. But it wasn't an entirely unpleasant feeling. That's when I saw my spirit.

I am not a deeply religious man, but there, with my eyes closed, I saw my face, saw my body, floating above the bed, dressed in a baggy white shirt and pants. I lifted up one of my arms and reached toward the image as if to pull it back inside me, but no matter how hard I tried, I could not grab it. It was as if I were trying to catch a butterfly with my bare hands, and no matter how hard I tried and how quickly I snapped my arm, I couldn't grab it. The spirit was me, and to see my soul separated from my body was a harrowing and terrifying experience.

I opened my eyes in a cold sweat.

"Luv! Luv!" I screamed, using my nickname for Stacy. She had fallen asleep next to me. I told her about my vision.

In the darkest of moments, with tears running down her cheeks, we embraced and she pleaded with me, "Please don't leave me," before resolutely insisting, "We will fight this together."

"Take me to the hospital," I said.

And with that, Stacy hurriedly woke up the kids and grabbed the hospital discharge papers as I crawled my way to the driveway. We drove the mile to her mother's house and left the kids in safe hands before flooring it to Piedmont Hospital, just north of downtown Atlanta. When we arrived at Piedmont, she shared the notes from the Dallas hospital and detailed the past seventy-two hours to anyone who would listen. She even suggested that I needed another blood transfusion.

"I'm sorry," the doctor replied, "but there are just so many side effects and risks with a transfusion that we don't do them at this stage. Let's do some more tests."

Tests. I was beginning to hate that word. *Everyone wants to do tests! Why can't someone just tell me what the hell is going on?*

Later that Sunday, the doctor ordered a bone marrow biopsy for the following day, based on his concern with my low white blood cell count. It was the first time I had ever even heard of a bone marrow biopsy.

He explained to me that humans have both red bone marrow, which actively makes red blood cells, and yellow bone marrow, which contains fat cells. We all need sufficient levels of all marrow in our bodies to produce healthy blood and healthy white and red blood cells. Most red marrow in adults is found in flatter bones such as the pelvis and breastbone. To get an accurate measure of the level of bone marrow in a patient, doctors have only one method of testing: extracting the marrow directly out of the bone.

I had on my hospital gown as the hematologist and a nurse came into the room and explained the procedure to me. They had me gingerly turn over onto my side on the hospital bed. They cleaned a small area on my lower back and gave me a shot of lidocaine to help numb what they told me might be extreme pain. I grabbed Stacy's hand.

The next thing I knew, I felt a sharp prick, then a stab, then pain like I had never experienced as the needle was screwed deep into the core of my pelvic bone. I winced and screamed out a few expletives. The initial needle insertion hurt, but not nearly as much as the aspiration, where the doctor literally sucked the marrow out of me, filling vial after vial. I could feel the marrow fluid leaving my body.

Most hospitals have an on-site lab that can turn around test results within twenty-four to forty-eight hours, so we knew we would have to wait. During that time, the doctors still refused to give me a transfusion.

That Sunday night, I called Craig and kept it brief. I shared with him that the doctor in Dallas had noted that it could be leukemia and that I had already had multiple blood transfusions. He mostly listened, and when I hung up, I thought that the call had been too short.

My whole life has been on the go. I can't stand sitting around, let alone being confined to a hospital, I thought to myself as I lay in bed. I passed the time joking with Stacy, watching television, and, when I could, sleeping. I thought about missing work, I thought about Stacy, and I thought about my kids. But as panicked as I felt after my encounter with Spirit Craig, and as painful as the bone marrow biopsy was, I felt strangely calm. I had somehow convinced myself that I had some sort of viral infection that we would laugh about when it went away in a few days. That I would shortly be back on the road as the NBA regular season drew to a close.

For her part, Stacy went right to work. She spent hours Googling potential diagnoses and treatments on her phone and called her mother, who had worked for the American College of Surgeons in Chicago and knew a lot about everything.

Those few days of waiting would turn out to be the worst of many days of waiting. Waiting for nurses to take my blood pressure. Waiting for doctors to make their rounds. Waiting to get tests and then waiting to get the results.

Finally, on Thursday morning, April 17, the hematologist who had done the biopsy walked in holding a clipboard and wearing a smile.

"Great news," he said, beaming. "The bone marrow is clean."

"Yes!" said Stacy, raising her hands in victory before leaning over to plant a kiss on the top of my head.

"This may just be an infection. I really see no reason to keep you here," the doctor continued. "I think we can discharge you today. Let's see how you do the next few days."

I was going home. Not only that, but I could get back on a

sideline somewhere without delay. Stacy called her mother to let her know we were coming home and began to gather my clothes. Of course, this was a hospital, so it could take hours before we were actually discharged, but Stacy's dancelike movements as she enthusiastically packed our stuff, checked, and rechecked the room could've entertained me for hours.

Around 4:00 p.m., the door opened. It was the hematologist again, this time looking grim.

"Mr. Sager," he said solemnly, "I am sorry. There has been a mistake. You have leukemia." He explained that in addition to sending the biopsy specimens to the lab at Piedmont, he had also sent them to Emory University Hospital, which has much more advanced technology for examining DNA sequencing. Emory diagnosed leukemia.

I looked over at Stacy and saw fear in her eyes.

"We are not a leukemia hospital," the doctor continued, "so you'll need to go to Emory or Northside Hospital for treatment. I have an ambulance ready to take you."

Both Emory and Northside are good hospitals. Emory is a teaching hospital and has some of the best doctors in the Southeast, with innovative clinical trials, and I knew close friends who had been treated there, including my Turner colleague Ernie Johnson. But Emory was farther into downtown Atlanta than Northside, and I naively believed that my family and friends wouldn't drive down that far to visit me, so I insisted on Northside and its medical team.

An ambulance transported me on a stretcher to Northside Hospital on the evening of April 17. I can remember everything about that ambulance ride—the EMT's face, the IV tubes, the dozens of instruments secured to the walls. I wished they could have driven me home to see my kids. For one of the only times in my life, I was scared. My whole world had been turned upside down in a matter of days. I didn't know what lay ahead of me; I didn't know what the hell leukemia was; I didn't know if I could go back to work.

During the twenty-minute ride from Piedmont to Northside, I could see out the two small back windows of the ambulance. Stacy was following us down the highway. I had wanted her to ride with me in the ambulance, but she drove herself instead, wanting to be able to have a car at the hospital. As tears poured down my cheeks, I blew kisses and waved to her from the back of the ambulance. But she made no acknowledgment. Seeing this left me feeling so alone and scared. I was overwhelmed with grief when we arrived at Northside and immediately asked Stacy why she hadn't waved back, and she explained that the windows were tinted on the outside and she just couldn't see anything going on inside the ambulance. There were no tears, no laughs, just whispers of fear of the unknown.

As soon as we arrived, I was wheeled directly up to the Blood and Marrow Transplant isolation floor. The thought that came to mind was: *Jail.*

Patients on the BMT floor are in dire health and have weakened immune systems that the tiniest of germs can attack with lethal consequences. The floor has its own air conditioning filtration system, and each of the thirty-six rooms can be sealed. No flowers, no balloons—nothing that can bring germs in. Just to access the floor, one must thoroughly wash hands and adorn a fresh hospital gown, a mask, a cap, shoe coverings, and a pair of latex gloves. As you might imagine, very few people are allowed on the floor. Patients, of course, and select nurses and doctors, but visitors are limited, and no children under the age of twelve are allowed, which included Riley and Ryan.

Stacy and I waited anxiously in a fairly large corner room with a window as nurses came in and went out, taking my vital signs—temperature, blood pressure, etc.

"We will go over everything with you as you get settled," a nurse said, "but get comfortable. You'll be here for thirty days, minimum." She said it so matter-of-factly that I almost missed it.

Thirty days?

It was like a prison sentence for an innocent man incarcerated for a crime he didn't commit. I was being punished for something that I didn't do.

"Mr. Sager," said a white coat, extending his hand toward me as he entered the room at 11:30 p.m., "I'm Dr. Holland." He shook Stacy's hand and then got right to it. "We need to start treating you immediately, and that means we must begin a round of chemotherapy to try to make some progress against the disease. Your levels," he said, and paused, "are not good."

"Doctor," I blurted out, making eye contact with Stacy, "I want to go home for the night. I need to see my kids." I was not mentally prepared to start treatment right away and get stuck in a hospital room for thirty days.

Dr. Holland looked at me, confused, and then turned to Stacy, as if to garner support for the idea that my leaving the hospital was nuts.

"Mr. Sager, I don't think you understand. We have everything all set up, and you need to start now. I can't force you to stay, but if you leave, we need to start the whole process all over again."

"I am going home," I insisted forcefully. "I will not stay here tonight."

Seeing that he wouldn't win, the doctor relented, and with that, I agreed to return to the hospital early in the morning to begin my treatment. I was only going to be away from the hospital for a few hours, but even one minute at home with Stacy, Riley, and Ryan was worth it.

Stacy and I drove home in the middle of the night on the dark highways of Atlanta in virtual silence.

"No way am I going to stay thirty days," I said, breaking the ice. "I will be out in nineteen."

As we pulled into the driveway, I felt better; fine, almost. I had regained my strength, which was why I was perplexed that I could feel and look fine but have this awful disease inside of me.

A few hours earlier, Craig had let the world in on my condition through a tweet, and my phone immediately began to ring incessantly. He hadn't asked me if he should, or even informed me that he would. But in a way, I was relieved that everyone knew, so I did not have to pretend that everything was fine and make up excuses for missing a game.

Stacy and I got a few hours of sleep and were up early the next day to get the kids ready for school. Ryan and Riley and I sat at the kitchen table, and I was honest with them. Their dad was sick and had to go to the hospital for treatment for a few weeks, and they wouldn't be able to come visit him. The kids were accustomed to my being on the road for weeks at a time with work, so their reaction to the news was to approach it like another work trip. I don't think that at the time, at ages seven and nine, they fully understood what I was telling them—but quite frankly, neither did I.

"Does this mean you can't come to lunch?" Ryan asked, keenly aware of our weekly tradition of having lunch together at school. It broke my heart.

Stacy and I drove the kids the half mile to school. I got out of the car and hugged them both harder than I ever had. I didn't know when I would get to hug them again. I tried to be brave for their sake, as if the hospital stay were no big deal. As they walked away from the car, tears were not only pooling in my eyes, they were streaming down my face. I looked at Stacy, and she was crying as well.

9

HIGH HOPES

As we had promised, we arrived at Northside Hospital early in the morning on Friday, April 18. I was struck by just how crowded the hospital was. The waiting rooms were packed, the hospital rooms were full, there were sick people everywhere. We made our way up to the Blood and Marrow Transplant floor. When the elevator doors opened, I took a deep breath as I followed Stacy out.

The first day was kind of a blur. I was shuffled from sterile room to sterile room. First to have my blood pressure and temperature taken, then to undergo another very painful bone marrow biopsy, then to have my blood drawn. I started out interested in what was happening, but I eventually settled on being a human pincushion and crash test dummy, and getting my education from brochures the hospital had given us that read like "Acute Myeloid Leukemia (AML) for Dummies."

Perfect.

Leukemia is, simply, a cancer of the bone marrow. When

we are a fetus inside our mother's womb, our spleen and liver produce our healthy red and white blood cells and our platelets, but when we're born, our bone marrow takes over production. Our red blood cells are critical, as they supply oxygen and nutrients to our body, and our platelets help our blood to clot and heal wounds. A healthy adult has 150,000 to 450,000 platelets at any given time, 4,500 to 11,000 white blood cells per microliter, and 4.5 million to 6 million red blood cells.

Leukemia attacks the blood system, and acute myeloid leukemia, which is what I was diagnosed with, creates a rapid reduction in healthy blood cells. AML usually builds over the course of a few weeks, and most symptoms reveal themselves moderately at first—fatigue, a fever, excessive bleeding. There are no cures for AML, beyond a stem cell transplant, and even then the odds are not great. It's been more than thirty years since any new treatments for the disease were approved by the Food and Drug Administration.

So what causes AML? Doctors still do not know. Some believe exposure to the chemical benzene, a by-product of cigarette smoke, can trigger it. But we do know what AML does in a typical patient: it changes. It mutates. Just when doctors feel they have found the right medicine to kill or slow the disease, the leukemia fights back by changing its makeup. Chemotherapy attacks a specific area, but after a while that area becomes immune to the effects of the chemo and the cycle starts over again. Eventually, most patients with AML in the advanced stage die from infection, bleeding, hemorrhaging, or systematic failure of the heart or lungs.

One of the positive things that I learned from the reading material was that Northside had a 100 percent one-year survival rate for AML patients, the best in the country. That's the kind of statistic that I love. But AML kills about ten thousand men and women every year, with close to twenty thousand new cases diagnosed every year, and the five-year survival rate is less than 25 percent.

"Three years" is what the doctors at Northside initially gave me. Three years on the outside, and that's only if I got the right kind of treatment and the best care and didn't get an infection and could have a successful transplant and my body took chemo well.

Three years. *Bull. I am living another thirty*, I thought.

I had to do the NBA playoffs in a few weeks, and then the PGA Championship, and then the baseball playoffs. My plate was already full for 2014.

"Denial" is a funny word. We're all living in denial to some extent. And even though it's fair to say I was living in denial regarding my diagnosis, the fighter mentality kicked in. I knew leukemia was serious, but I never thought it would defeat me or challenge me as much as it has. And yet I think I am even *more* optimistic and positive in my outlook now.

Statistics are just numbers, and you can take from them what you want to see. I've been a gambler my whole life, and I know all about odds. I will bet on anything. A shot in golf, a game of Go Fish, the number of beers I can drink in five minutes. It makes me feel alive. I have been known to make cross-country trips to Las Vegas to play a little craps and wager in the sports books and then be home by dinner. In fact, over most of my career, I mandated that any time I flew west of the Mississippi River, I had to have a layover in Vegas.

Sometimes I can't tell the difference between a realist and a pessimist. So when a pessimist or realist tells me the odds of my surviving with leukemia are low, I think about Stacy. I take a step back and think about the odds of a fifty-something divorced father of three, who Kevin Garnett once said looked like a Christmas ornament, having a shot with a woman who, as you'd find out if you're lucky enough to meet her, is even more beautiful inside than she is outside. If there was ever a time to be grateful for inheriting my mother's joie de vivre, this is it.

I bet on me.

So with that optimism and resolve, I began my fight with leukemia in a corner room with a five-day dose of chemotherapy. Most adults have heard horror stories about chemotherapy and its side effects—nausea, vomiting, hair loss, weight loss—and I knew well what I was facing. Interestingly, "getting chemo" is really just having an IV in your arm. The chemo is a mixture of medications—some of them toxic—that doctors use to kill off the leukemia cells. Surprisingly, in those first few days—and, in fact, throughout my fight—I have been fortunate enough to not feel many of the side effects. No nausea or vomiting, though there has been hair loss after some intense chemo.

Over the first few days, Stacy educated herself in the world of cancer, asking questions of doctors and nurses, consulting over the phone with doctors she knew and didn't know, and spending hours researching treatment options and experimental drugs. She figured that doctors in all fields barely touched the surface of the options available to them, and she always insisted on multiple opinions when it came to health. I never had the urge to ask a lot of questions about the disease or the future—ironic, I know, because my entire life I have been curious and my profession has groomed me to be inquisitive. Maybe

I was in denial. Maybe I knew that as long as Stacy knew, I was fine. All I wanted to know was what the doctors wanted me to do to get better. I want to live to see Ryan win Wimbledon and Riley invent the next groundbreaking technology. I want to walk Krista down the aisle and watch Craig and Kacy write their magnum opuses. I want to have many more years left to enjoy life with Stacy, and I want to get back on the sidelines to witness history.

I was uplifted when my three oldest kids came to visit in those first few days. I put on a strong face, as they were not used to seeing their father so vulnerable, and I tried to steer the conversation toward their work or sports, but I could tell from their faces that they had other things on their minds. They didn't know it, but I could see my daughters burst into tears the minute they exited my room. It broke my heart. I couldn't stand the sight of my children in pain or worrying.

In the first few days of my hospitalization, Marv Albert, Charles Barkley, Ernie Johnson, and Kenny Smith all visited me at Northside, of course wearing the required garments and accessories—gown, shoe covers, mask, gloves, and cap—all of which looked hysterical on Charles. Text messages and phone calls from everyone from Phil Mickelson to NBA commissioner Adam Silver buoyed my spirits, as did a huge flower bouquet from Kevin Garnett. I even received a letter from a chicken.

> *Dear Craig,*
> *Jane and I hope this card finds you further along in your success to recovery. Millions of people love you and we trust you are feeling the warmth of that glow.*
> *Your fortitude is boundless! But then, you've proven that with your jackets, my friend! This is your championship time,*

Craig. And Coach Pop will be interviewing you about your win soon.

We love you, Craig.
Ted & Jane Giannoulas

Ted was the original San Diego Chicken.

But the most surprising and moving act of kindness that I received in those first few weeks would come not from a colleague or a friend, but rather from my namesake.

10

A New Normal

Tracking my father's work schedule was an innate skill in the Sager family. His fleeting homecomings were a weekly game to see how much we could squeeze in before his spasmodic circuit around the country continued. Each day was its own battle in our perpetual war with time, but the month of April was in a league of its own. By the time the NCAA Tournament wrapped up in early April, there was one golden week for us to spend time together, chart the next two and a half months, and restock the wardrobe, because the NBA playoffs were around the corner.

Phone calls have always connected his world with mine, and over the years we've drifted further and further away from a standard dialogue. A compressed vernacular developed that kept us informed at light speed. We could turn weeks of our lives into an elevator pitch of information that only another Sager would be able to understand and reassemble. We'd recap the previous night's game with a single exchange. Context clues weren't necessary for understanding the humor or purpose of a story. By the second ring of my phone, I could guess where he was probably calling from based on the time of day. From this I could deduce what game he was covering and exactly what I needed to update him about since our last conversation.

Then I got the call that changed everything.

Almost a week had passed since Shabazz Napier and the Connecticut Huskies had defeated Kentucky in the 2014 NCAA national championship game. I expected my dad to arrive home, or at least be on his way home, after his NBA game in Dallas on the 10th. But now, three days later, it was Masters Sunday, and the playoffs were just seven days away. After rushing to a television to watch the final hole of Bubba Watson's second title at Augusta, my girlfriend gave me a concerned look and said, "You need to call your dad. I don't know what it is, but I have a bad feeling that something is wrong."

I looked at her like she was crazy. I had called him earlier that day and gotten his voice mail, but I wasn't concerned. Phone tag was another inborn skill in our family. I reminded her that he was watching the exact same thing we were and that I would call him after Bubba put on the green jacket. Minutes later, however, it was my phone that was ringing. The real-time reaction to Bubba's victory that I was expecting to hear from Dad was instead "I've been in a Dallas hospital for three days and just arrived at Piedmont today."

The only other words I remember are "It could be leukemia" and "I've already had six blood transfusions."

Hearing the word "leukemia" come out of my father's mouth was a punch in the stomach. I felt my entire world change before I could catch my breath. I knew that leukemia was a blood cancer and that it was a devastating disease, and hearing that he had already had six blood transfusions, I recognized that it must be serious. I had never seen my father go to the doctor in my entire life, let alone heard him mention anything about his health. He was in phenomenal condition and still ran miles every day. What were we in for?

I rushed to the hospital to see him. The very thought of his vulnerability in any capacity was all I could stress about as I hurried through the hallways and counted down the room numbers racing by me.

When I opened the half-closed door, the scene was like a flash of lightning that I could feel getting stored away in my memory. As I looked at my father lying down in a hospital bed for the first time, it was heartbreaking. I couldn't tell if it was his being hospitalized or his being absolutely exhausted that I found more upsetting. Understanding that these symptoms stemmed from the same greater danger made it even more unbearable. I walked over to the bed and gave him a half-hug, not wanting to accidently disconnect the various tubes running into his body. I used all my senses to find a clue as to what I should and could do next.

Dad launched into a CliffsNotes version of his terrifying journey back to Georgia. I had a million questions, and I wasn't sure if I should just ask all of them or wait for another day.

So much of my life had been shaped by the fast pace of life we shared together. There was always the next game feeding our excitement. The seasons never stopped, and the cycle was always leading us a step ahead. The wayward world of sports was my circadian rhythm. Now, I was in an uncharted reality that couldn't have felt any more backward.

He pointed to the television in the upper corner of his dimly lit room. I hadn't looked at what was on the television since walking in, but as soon as I saw the Yankees and Red Sox on *Sunday Night Baseball*, he started to catch me up on the last two innings.

The gravity of the situation relaxed its grip the moment I accepted his invitation to a conversation about sports and nothing else. It was hollow commentary on a game I had no interest in at the time, but I knew exactly how meaningful this was for us. We watched until he started to doze off, and I left knowing that no matter what was about to happen, we'd always have sports.

For the next three days, we waited for any sort of metric to define the severity of his leukemia and the subsequent treatment plan. Not having a game plan was an emotional high-wire act. One negative thought and I'd free-fall into the hypotheticals and worst-case scenarios. I had lost two beloved aunts to cancer right when I'd gotten to college, and now there was a magnifying glass over those tender scars again. My sisters and I were rallying together, and there was a positive bond of support growing between us, but that is a thorny mind-set to guard when so much is left unknown.

Since I had learned of the diagnosis on Sunday, I kept thinking about the upcoming NBA playoffs, which was my dad's time to shine. It felt strange to be worrying about his job in the middle of the forbidding reality around me, but I understood more than most that my father's work was not merely a job—it was the air that he breathed. Just the thought of having that taken away from him scared me more than leukemia. His love of sports, his energy, and his insatiable craving for excitement are what keep my dad going, at a pace I can't keep up with even on my best days. He is himself in the purest form, and I didn't know how I could possibly make him feel better as he was about to miss out on the most exciting time of the year.

Thursday evening, he called with his initial game plan. I was relieved, but also reminded of what a long road lay ahead. He was beginning a three-to-six-week chemotherapy treatment cycle the next morning at Northside Hospital, just minutes away from my office. I could tell from his voice and his words that reality had started to set in, but he was grounded with confidence and a new focus. I assured him I'd be there in the morning to check on him, and we ended the call. I let another opportunity go by without telling him all the things I wanted to say. Not talking about my fears was clearly the preferred strategy, but it had been four days and I felt like the only contribution I had made was worrying and simply offering my presence. I wanted to do more.

The three-to-six-week chemo plan confirmed that he was going to miss the entire playoffs, and it gave me a general idea of what was on the horizon. I wished that night that someone at Turner would call and ask me to fill in for him. I wanted the name Craig Sager to make an appearance at some point during the postseason to keep his playoff streak alive. Though I had been working as a writer and editor, I had no on-air experience. No one in his or her right mind would trust me to do what I was obsessively thinking about. I didn't even trust myself to do it. But if there was ever going to be a time to step up and be the real Craig Sager for a day, the clock was ticking.

I stared deeply into the picture I kept on my desk at work, of him and me "hosting" *Inside the NBA* together in 1989. This had been my first and only television appearance. He recapped the night's action while I sat in my high chair holding a basketball and gobbling the M&M's that my mother was sneaking onto my tray from underneath the anchor desk to keep me smiling. This is the image that had replayed in my head all these years when he would leave home to venture off to his next big game. I pictured a time in the future when it would be the two Sager men working side by side. That picture represented the life I felt I was born to pursue. This picture got me through sleepless nights working in empty offices and long drives through the middle of the night from high school gyms.

I had a difficult decision to make. I didn't want my dad's absence at the playoffs to be the clue that something was wrong. That was a sad and unavoidable reality. *Surely there must be something I can do*, I thought to myself. The rumors would spread like wildfire if the media got ahold of this first, I reasoned. Motivated to do something, I composed a tweet, with a collage of pictures of my father's life off of the sidelines with my sisters and me.

My Dad's 3–4 week acute leukemia treatment starts tmrw. Be thinking of him & let's get him back on the sidelines soon.

For over an hour I stared at my phone and walked around my house trying to figure out if I should push SEND. I had a general idea of the speed that news can travel on social media. My chronic fear of nepotism that could shade all the work I've put in over the years gave me doubts about whether or not I should get in the middle of this unknown journey ahead. Then I asked myself, "What would my dad do if he were me?" At 7:46 p.m., I sent it.

I felt responsible for the barrage of questions that employees of Turner and other members of the sports media were about to be blindsided by. My Twitter account was the only source to go by at the time, and that's a dangerous game to play. But rather than the political onslaught I anticipated, we received an outpouring of support that was inspiring. The sports world rallied behind the world's biggest sports fan, and he walked into his treatment the next morning with more support and momentum than any of us could have dreamed of.

Day one of my father's treatment brought a new wave of the unexpected. The news of his diagnosis was out, and now my focus shifted back to what my role would be. Having my father stationed right down the road from me for a long period was a hard concept to grasp. I wasn't used to knowing exactly where he was at all times. I started to wonder what this would mean for our relationship. Sacrificing family time for work was the natural order of things—the whole family had been guilty of that. Was this our reset button to discover a new way of life? I was finally going to get to catch up with my dad. I could watch the NBA playoffs with him and tap into his knowledge in real time. We were going to get the father-son time that we had been too busy to get before. Maybe there was something positive that could come out of this—it became the only thing that I wanted.

When I got to the bone marrow floor, I entered the

sanitation corridor that kept his wing sealed off from the outside world. The potpourri of sanitizer and latex permeating the space was a reminder of how uncomfortable hospitals made me. I took a deep breath of the sterilized air and let it fill my chest. It was time to get over it. I reached for the stack of blue hospital gowns and then slipped on the matching shoe covers. The first set of doors closed behind me as I tied the gown. I stepped toward the second set of double doors separating me from my father's new home and completed the checklist by securing my surgical mask. I got greenlighted to press a metal plate, and doors slowly opened, revealing a freeway of nurses, doctors, and patients who were all moving with purpose.

I scanned my surroundings and found myself face-to-face with a wall of informational pamphlets on leukemia next to the family waiting room. Seeing those for the first time really stung. I was reminded how oblivious I was to the complexity of this disease and how much time and effort my medical illiteracy was going to need to be rectified. I made my way to the far corner of the floor, where his spacious room with plenty of windows waited.

Dad raised his arm and gave me a fist bump and a "Let's do this." Every bit of his focus was on beating leukemia, staying positive, and getting back on the sideline. I could see the endless supply of strength and determination that had been exhausted earlier that week. He was back.

Tara August, vice president of talent relations at Turner, came in to visit my dad the minute after I walked in the room. After setting down a massive stack of magazines for us, she applauded the amazing support he had received. She pulled out her phone and showed my dad the Keith

Olbermann piece that had aired the night before on ESPN2, after my tweet, a segment detailing my father's boldness and positive outlook on life, ending with the words "Leukemia picked the wrong opponent."

Tara and I were in tears watching him see it for the first time. His smile grew as the video continued, until the dramatic ending we were waiting for him to hear.

"Wow," he howled before jumping in the air and going around the room for a round of high-fives. The short-lived delight ended when a doctor came in to start an hour-long procedure and asked us to step outside. Tara met me in the hallway.

"We have an idea," she said. "How would you like to go to San Antonio tomorrow and interview Coach Popovich in place of your dad for Sunday's game?"

"That would be a dream come true," I responded, with complete sincerity and the overwhelming astonishment I was experiencing.

She called the Spurs, and I could hear her ask Popovich if he would be okay with a sit-down interview Sunday morning before the 1:00 p.m. tip-off with the Dallas Mavericks. She nodded to me and put her thumb up when he said yes.

"Don't worry," Tara assured me. It will be taped, so we can edit it and do it over again if we need to. Just make sure your father doesn't find out." Turner wanted it to be an uplifting surprise for him.

I managed to hide my bewilderment, excitement, and nervousness when I returned to his room. After a few more minutes, I plainly told him he would see me again this weekend, and I said goodbye. That afternoon, Tara e-mailed me my flight details and let me know that a car service would pick me up first thing in the morning. Yet I now faced a true Sager conundrum.

What was I going to wear?

I drove up to my dad's house in Canton that night to try to pick out an outfit. I never knew what he was going to wear at a game. His style is his creation, and I'm usually just as shocked as the rest of the world watching. He had more than ninety blazers in his closet, what seemed like four hundred ties, and I could not even estimate the number of dress shirts, which came in every shade, texture, and pattern imaginable. I mixed and matched and tried to find something that would sit between his current style and something he would have worn when he was my age. I sat on the floor of the closet, clothes surrounding me.

I remembered all the combinations that I had seen him wear before, and I wanted to find something new. Finally, I found one jacket that still had a tag hanging from it. He never wears the same outfit on the air twice, and this would allow me to christen a new jacket for him. It was charcoal gray with a maroon-and-orange windowpane pattern and felt like the perfect blend of my unadorned fashion sense and his. I had a groovy $9 pair of maroon velvet pants and I was set.

Once I landed in San Antonio on Saturday, I attended the production meeting with producer Craig Silver and the rest of the crew. We planned out the broadcast and talked specifics on how my sit-down would go with Coach Popovich, all the while sharing stories about my dad. I tried my best to hide how nervous I really was. I also had to convince them that I had a plan for my shaggy red hair, which hadn't been cut in over a year. The nicknames—like "Thor" and "Ginger Clay Matthews"—that I heard on a daily basis amused me, but I wanted to hide my shoulder-length locks as much as possible. I told the crew not to worry, confident that I'd figure something out.

After the production meeting, I made a beeline for the River Walk (Paseo del Rio), a five-mile-long public walkway along the San Antonio River, full of restaurants, bars, and shops. The first father-son trip we ever had was to San Antonio, for the Western Conference finals in 2003, when I was a teenager, and I had fallen in love with the city. The two of us returned to the Alamo City nine years later for the 2012 Western Conference finals and hit up the River Walk for the first time as adults. I remembered all the bars we went to, and I made my way down to our go-to spot, Mad Dogs, to do exactly what my dad would do as a twenty-five-year-old version of himself covering the playoffs.

I ordered my first Bud Light of the night and soaked in the live music and excitement around me. I was back in San Antonio partying at the River Walk. I had to call my dad and tell him, but before I even reached for my phone, I caught myself and remembered I was on a clandestine operation. For the first time in my life, I realized what life would be like if I were unable to call him. It felt real. I experienced complete emptiness and my whole body ached. I felt like I had been dropped into the bottom of the ocean. Having no one to share that night with gave me the loneliest feeling I had ever felt. But I realized that the biggest day of my life was ahead of me and tried to let that keep me occupied.

The next morning, I had a job to do. I woke up and

went straight for a run on the River Walk like my dad did every morning before his games. Thankfully, it was an early Easter Sunday tip-off, and I had only a couple of unnerving hours before I was on my way to AT&T Center. I started to get dressed and attempted to put my hair up in a ponytail for the first time. My father was never a fan of my hair, and every day at least one person told me to cut it. I wanted to donate my hair to cancer patients in honor of my aunts, and I still had a long way to go, so cutting it wasn't an option. Of course, I hadn't been expecting to be on television anytime soon, either. I brought out the two hair ties that I had snatched from my family's bathroom before I'd left and strained muscles and tendons that I didn't know I had in order to reach back and lock down the perfect ponytail. My arms were burning, and I made sure nothing touched my head for the next five hours while avoiding making any sudden movements. I gained a whole new perspective on what women have to deal with.

Fully dressed now, I went down to the hotel lobby and hopped in a car with Reggie Miller, who was also catching a ride to the arena to provide color commentary for the game.

"Oh, yeah, I love it, Sages," laughed Reggie, using my dad's nickname, when he saw the getup.

We got to the arena just before 10:00 a.m., thirty minutes before my scheduled sit-down with Popovich. I had no idea what was about to happen or even what we were going to talk about, as the game had yet to be played. I stood in the hallway minutes before the interview, with a camera crew ready to set up and start rolling the second Popovich rounded the corner. Talking to Popovich was actually the only thing I *wasn't* worried about. I loved him from afar, my family admired him, and playing college football had long ago squashed my fear of any imposing coach.

I felt like a contestant on *Who Wants to Be a Millionaire?* except there was no million dollars, and no lifelines to keep me from looking like an idiot on national television.

Popovich came out of his office and introduced himself. He was much taller in person than I had thought, and his strong hand shook mine as we exchanged hellos. He mentioned to the crew that he wanted to speak with me in private for a moment, and I followed him into his office and took a seat across from his desk as he closed the door.

"Craig, I want you to know how much I respect your dad," he began, and followed with details of his admiration and an instruction.

"If you aren't taking care of your responsibilities, you aren't going to be able to take care of those around you. Make sure you do what you need to do."

Then he leaned over and handed me a handwritten letter that he wanted me to give to my dad when I got home.

I was still wondering when we were going get this interview over with.

"Oh, and I don't want to tape this thing," Pop said, matter-of-factly. "That won't work. Let's do this live after the third quarter, just like your dad would."

This was Popovich's idea and no one else's. It hadn't come up once in Turner discussions, and no one asked him to do it. I was going to literally fill in for my father, and it was Popovich making the call. It would be special, but . . . wait. It would be *live* on national television! What started as a tribute had just become my chance to experience a lifelong dream and something truly life-changing.

Nervously, I agreed, and Pop and I exchanged hugs. As we left his office, I told the surprised crew about the change of plans. I wondered if I even had the authority to accept Pop's proposal, but I remembered who was standing next to me.

Since the original plan had been to be done with this long before tip-off, I was supposed to be sitting in the stands and not on press row during the game. Now, with the change in plans, I would move from the stands down to the court at the start of the third quarter and share a seat with sideline reporter Jaime Maggio, who would also make sure I was where I needed to be for my "hit."

During the pregame show on TNT, host and friend Ernie Johnson teased my upcoming appearance during the game. At the time, I had no idea if my father was watching, though I assumed he would be. As the game went on, I became more and more nervous. *What the hell am I doing?* But I thought about all of the lessons that I have learned from my father, about using your brains to figure things out, and about a willingness to be different, and then I thought about how he would have handled this situation. He would have found a way to make it work, and I would do the same.

As the quarter ended, I stood under the basket, ready to run out to the spot on the floor Jaime had pointed out to me, where I should meet Coach Popovich. Jaime was instructed by the truck to open the interview and then hand the microphone to me to take over. The horn sounded, and I rushed to the designated mark, dodging cords, cheerleaders, and the chaos all around me.

Popovich walked over and was surprised to see Jaime.

"I thought Junior was doing this?"

"He is," answered Jaime. "We're going to throw it to him."

"No, just hand him the mic," he ordered. "Don't complicate this."

I grabbed the mic and looked for a cue or something to tell me what the hell was happening. I stared at the camera, having no idea when to start talking, or even if I was already on live television. I had no earpiece to hear the truck for my cue. It was just Pop and me out there together, in the eye of the storm that I felt circling around me.

"Five seconds," warned Jaime, out of camera range. I started a countdown in my head. It was so loud I could barely think.

"It's a tie game in San Antonio," I opened as Popovich watched with a grin. When I saw his face, I felt safe, and the bliss of the moment took over. It turned into a quick "How's it going, it's nice to see you" as I tried to regain my focus and stop smiling long enough to ask my questions.

"How would you assess your team's performance so far?" was my first question. "What do you need to do in the fourth quarter to pull away and close this one out?" was the second.

Pop took it easy on me and actually answered my questions, and I just focused on keeping a steady hand and not letting the microphone shake. My feet were shaking with adrenaline, and my legs were starting to as well. Then, Pop looked directly into the camera.

"Craig, we miss ya. You've been an important part of all of this for a long time, doing a great job. We want your fanny back on the court, and I promise I'll be nice."

He patted me on the shoulder, told me "Good job," and was on the bench coaching his team seconds later.

I was processing what had just happened as we were told to clear the court. I looked up at the packed arena and captured the moment in my mind. I treasured each step I was taking in my father's shoes, and it was a mesmerizing experience. Big moments and big interviews are what my dad has fearlessly done his entire career. Now I had one.

11

POP

G regg Popovich has never really liked the press and does pre-game and postgame press conferences and interviews only because it is mandated by the NBA—and even then, he tends to respond with a scowl or, at best, one- or two-word answers. Now he has to do *in-game* interviews as well, so you can imagine how much he loves those.

Our interviews after games became legendary, as Pop's body language and curt responses to my questions made for a really taut relationship. In 2003, when I was covering the Olympic trials in Puerto Rico and Pop was an assistant coach on the team, we ran into each other in the hotel lobby. We exchanged pleasantries—I could tell that he didn't have much interest in talking with me, but I engaged him in a personal conversation. In retrospect, maybe I saw this chance meeting as an opportunity to break the ice. I let him know that he and I had almost been teammates at the Air Force Academy, that if not for my appointment to West Point instead of Colorado Springs, I would have been a cadet with him. As I talked, his lips reluctantly curled upward into a smile, and his contributions to the dialogue grew to three or sometimes *four* words, and when we parted ways, he gave me a smile and a handshake that felt genuine.

Years later, during the 2012–13 season, while covering a San Antonio–Oklahoma City game, I listened in as Pop ripped into Tony Parker during a timeout. After the game, I asked Parker on-air about the tirade. The next day at the NBA's mandatory meetings between coaches and broadcasters, Pop laid into me in front of Marv Albert and my colleagues. He called me an "ambulance chaser" and threatened to never speak with me again for asking Parker about Pop's tirade. He then insisted that he wouldn't share any information with Marv or the crew anymore.

At the shootaround before the game, Pop did his typical media press conference. I tried to grab him for a minute to apologize, but he wanted nothing to do with me, so I took some paper, scribbled an apology, and handed it to him on his way out. He took it, gave me the Pop scowl, and continued on his way.

Now, in 2014, as I lay in a hospital bed in Atlanta, Pop once again was in my life. I didn't see the TNT pregame show, so I did not know that Junior would be making an appearance until halftime, when Ernie teased it again. I couldn't believe it. Junior had just been in my room that weekend and had said nothing to me about it. But my shock turned to a father's nervousness for his kid. Would he ask the right questions? Would he understand the director's cues in his earpiece? *Would Pop be kind?*

The next thirty minutes, I was a nervous wreck. I knew the interview would come at the end of the third quarter. I wanted to call Junior beforehand, but something held me back. I lay in the hospital bed, IVs attached, chemo flowing into my veins, with Stacy next to me, recording my reaction.

We watched the interview. Tears rolled down my cheeks. I was so enormously proud of the way Junior handled it, as he had no on-air experience at all. But beyond that, the gesture of his willingness to step in for me brought me immense pride. I had not felt that close to my son in many years.

When Junior returned the following day, he handed me a sealed, unaddressed envelope with the Spurs logo in the return address spot. I used what little strength I had to carefully open the envelope.

> *Craig,*
>
> *I heard the news and want you to know you are in our thoughts as you begin this process. It certainly will not be easy and I can only hope you will persevere and beat it.*
>
> *Your intellect, competitiveness and humor will certainly be good companions as you move forward at this difficult time.*
>
> *Bottom line, get your butt back on the court where you belong! We make a great team.*
>
> *Very Best, Pop*

It was a classy and unnecessary gesture by Pop, and it certainly gave me a boost in energy. I was going to make it back to the court no matter what. As I lay in bed, my fate uncertain, I thought back to the canvas of my career, and the moments that made it up. It had all started at a tiny radio station in Sarasota, Florida, with a call from a guy named Cliff.

12

THE COLORS OF MY LIFE

As my high school years were drawing to a close, and my realization that I was unlikely to become a professional athlete came to the forefront, I figured the best way to get my real-time rush of adrenaline coursing through my veins would be to become a professional fighter pilot in the Air Force. Ever since I'd watched the planes take off and land at O'Hare with my father, I'd been in love with planes, and besides, my father had served his country, so it was only fitting that I should as well. My parents were conflicted about my ambition to seek a nomination to the Air Force Academy in Colorado Springs—this was at the height of the Vietnam War.

My father wanted me to explore all my options, so we visited the University of Miami, where his buddy and WWII cohort, Bert Parks, was a distinguished alum. I got a taste of the Ivy League on the Dartmouth campus. And, of course, I spent time at Northwestern, my hometown school. The Academy nomination process played out, and I was informed that Representative Charlotte Reid had not nominated me to the Academy, but rather to the United States Military Academy—West Point. No airplanes, perhaps, but *not too shabby*, I thought to myself.

I took a visit to a cold and snowy West Point and met with a young basketball coach named Bobby Knight, who would go on to win nine hundred games at Army, Indiana, and Texas Tech and be enshrined in the Basketball Hall of Fame. At that time, he wasn't yet the volatile coach that he would come to be known as. (Years later, when Coach Knight and I became friends, I told him that I'd almost played for him at Army. "Sager," he responded, "what makes you think you would have played?") But after giving it some thought, I didn't want to become a soldier with a four-year postgraduate commitment to the Army, and I decided to attend Northwestern, which would conveniently also keep me near my Cubbies.

When I arrived at Northwestern in the late summer of 1969, I tried out for the Northwestern football team, despite my profound dislike of football practice. I was an athlete, and I couldn't imagine not playing a sport in the fall, so I tried out for the freshman team, since in those days freshmen were ineligible to play varsity. I suited up in full pads in the Chicago heat in August and took on guys who were my size (since I had finally grown a few inches), just with more football ability than me. During one preseason practice, I suffered a concussion returning kicks. Later that day, I suffered another concussion. As I lay on the field, I knew I was at Northwestern and I knew my name, but other than that I had no idea of anything else. At the hospital, they told me I had double amnesia and that I would need to wear a foam helmet around campus while riding a bike. No way. I decided to leave football behind before ever playing a game in college, and to focus my time on basketball, playing pickup at Patten Gym for hours on end. I had grown six inches since my senior year of high school, and with my ball-handling skills, I figured I had a decent shot of making the freshman team.

I introduced myself to the freshman coach, Jim Braegel, and asked for the chance to be a walk-on. Not only did I get the chance, but, after injuries to many of the team's key players, including star Rick Sund, I ended up playing significant minutes my freshman year, enough to earn a scholarship on the varsity team the following year—or so I thought. I loved the game, of course, but I also loved the camaraderie and the travel and the practices. I loved everything about playing basketball at Northwestern. Prior to the start of the next season, colleges changed the rules to allow freshmen to compete on varsity, which limited the number of spots for guys like me. Coach Brad Snyder said that I could practice with the team as a walk-on, but my playing time would be very limited. With the demands on a student-athlete and with a true desire to get my degree in four years, I decided to step away from basketball before my sophomore season.

Somehow, some way, I wanted to be around sports. It was like air to me. I did enjoy the spirit of the school, so I decided to join the Northwestern cheerleading squad, believing that I would get to go on the road with the team. But I soon learned that that wasn't the case. So in November, when there was an opening to be the school's mascot, Willie the Wildcat, I jumped at the chance, as Willie always went on the road—and didn't even have to practice during the week. Long story short, I got the job, and for the next two years, this Willie was perhaps a little too wild, as my "ask for forgiveness later" attitude got me in all sorts of trouble.

My first big football game as Willie happened at powerhouse Ohio State University, where the Wildcats were huge underdogs. I put everything I had into being an obnoxious, energetic, unabashed Wildcat supporter, albeit through my body motions and my enormous fake wildcat head. Unbelievably, Northwestern scored a dramatic upset in Columbus, and the Buckeye fans were not happy. It probably didn't help that I remained on the field, taunting the Ohio State fans and players and reveling in our victory after the game. It didn't take long for some members of the Ohio State marching band to begin pushing me and poking me with their flagpoles. Ohio State security couldn't care less. Somehow, word made it back to the Northwestern locker room, and dozens of players in full pads came to my rescue. It would be the first of my many escapades as Willie.

My love affair with my college of choice in no way compromised my devotion to the Chicago Cubs, and I made every effort to attend their games. In 1971, I was there in the left-center-field bleachers as my hero, Ernie Banks, stepped up to the plate at Wrigley, on the verge of hitting his five hundredth career home run. With a crack of the bat, the ball was headed my way. I was absolutely convinced that I would catch the historic ball. It was coming right toward me. *Down, down, down,* I stuck out my hands and . . . it eluded my fingers and landed just beyond the netting the Cubs had recently installed above the outfield brick-and-ivy wall and bounced back off the hard concrete of the stands. It was just one of many Cubs moments I was able to experience while I was in school at Northwestern.

As for my studies, I marched to the beat of my own drum. During my senior year, for example, I engaged in an independent study program with a young professor on campus, Gary Wodder. Along with two classmates, I wanted to study the effects that alcohol and marijuana consumption had on the motor skills of subjects, something with which we had *some* experience. So one day, we gathered in a campus gymnasium with twelve volunteer subjects. Before any substances were consumed, each of the twelve subjects—including me—was baseline-tested on speed, reflex time, endurance, and free-throw-shooting ability. (I made 24 of 30 initially.)

After all baseline tests had been recorded, all twelve subjects left with instructions—six to start drinking beer and six to smoke pot over the next four hours. It was only natural that I be included in the six who drank.

I went back to our fraternity house and started pounding beers. Four hours later, we all reconvened at the gym and were tested on the same metrics as before. I scored better in every test after drinking for four hours, including increasing my free throw percentage from 80 percent to 87 percent. (That research explains why I score better in golf as the round goes on.)

As graduation inched closer in June 1973, I had some choices to make. I could go back to Batavia, I could stay in Chicago, maybe even play some basketball in Belgium—one of my former teammates was now coaching overseas—or I could pursue a job doing what I did best: *talking*. My dream job was to do play-by-play for the Chicago Cubs, which seemed an unlikely goal, so instead I set my target on being a major-market television sports anchor. (Although I made a mental note after graduation that if I was not on television by the age of twenty-nine, I was going to become a race car driver. I craved the need for speed!)

My parents had moved down to Sarasota shortly after I graduated high school, and over the summers I had spent time working at local radio and television stations there. In fact, during the summer of 1972, the Democrats held their convention at the Miami Beach Convention Center, and the news director sent me to Miami to try to get some sound bites from delegates and politicians. Political talk was common around our dinner table, with Dad occasionally looking up from his work to chime in in defense of Richard Nixon, and I was fairly well-versed in the politics of the time. But during a hotly contested convention that resulted in the nomination of George McGovern for president, I got to see firsthand that politics was a combat sport and that the drama, competitiveness, and uncertainty that drew me to sports could be found in the political arena as well. But politics and news reporting was not in my future. I found news to be very conflicting: I had a very cheerful, happy personality, which made delivering depressing reports of murders, robberies, and scandals quite difficult. Whereas in sports I could witness triumphs and successes, and report on remarkable achievements.

Before my Northwestern graduation, Cliff Lanson, the station manager from WSPB Radio in Sarasota, offered me a job at $94 per week doing morning and afternoon news updates, and I accepted. I moved to Florida and began my new job, supplementing my income by giving sailing lessons on the waters of the Gulf and bouncing and bartending at Big Daddy's, a chain of bars in Florida that became an instant success with the lowering of the state's drinking age from twenty-one to eighteen in 1973. I became one of Big Daddy Flanigan's favorite employees and soon found myself in a management role, counting money and closing stores from Sarasota to Naples to Fort Lauderdale on the weekends.

I poured my heart into my radio job and took it very seriously, tracking down leads, showing up at city council meetings, and otherwise smothering the local news scene. In addition to the newscasts, I served as the host and play-by-play man of the local high school football scene, broadcasting a game of the week every Friday night. I didn't cover professional sports. That is, until 1974, when a major sports event came on the horizon and I knew that I had to be there to report on it.

———

Henry "Hank" Aaron had finished the 1973 season with 713 home runs, one shy of tying the great Babe Ruth, and Aaron endured the attention, as well as some racially motivated threats on his life, in the off-season. So, based on his contemporaneous output, the record-breaking homer was likely to come in the opening series in Cincinnati or during the home opener in Atlanta the following week. As a local radio news reporter in Sarasota, I wasn't assigned to the story, but as a baseball fanatic, I followed the home run chase closely, and when Aaron tied but did not break the record in Cincy, I knew that I had to be at the next game in Atlanta.

It just so happens that WSPB was a radio affiliate of the Atlanta Braves, so I knew many of the players and key staff. I used that angle when I asked my boss, Cliff, to allow me to travel there to report on Aaron potentially achieving this ground-breaking milestone. He thought about it for a few seconds.

"Be back for drive time in the morning," Cliff finally said, sternly, from across his desk—then, leaning in: "or you're fired."

I laughed. He didn't. Then I didn't. "Yes, sir . . . *Of course, sir* . . ."

I bought a ticket on National Airlines and flew directly from Sarasota to Atlanta the afternoon of the game. I had no game ticket, but I was reasonably confident that my connections in the Braves' public relations department would come through with a credential—which, God bless 'em, they did, but one that simply got me into the stadium. I wasn't the only journalist asking for a favor, and as I was not the highest on their priority list, they had no media seat for me, just the photographers' box next to the third-base dugout, and that's where I was relegated. So there I sat, field-side, packing light—it was just me and my microphone and recorder, next to a cameraman from NBC, which was nationally televising the game. I felt like Maury Wills, anxious for the steal sign . . .

Before the first pitch, on a cold and wet night when the weather nearly canceled the game, I was on the field, talking with managers and players from both teams, as well as with Aaron's parents. Back in those days, athletes and coaches were much more accessible and willing to talk with the media. As the game got started, I stood in the photographers' bay in one of my father's old white trench coats . . . waiting . . .

After a lifetime of memorizing statistics and achievements, I held Babe Ruth's 714 career home runs in reverence as the greatest milestone in sports, and I viewed Aaron's breaking the record as the greatest moment in the history of our national pastime. Feeling the moment, the tension, the anticipation of seeing the imagery of the flags waving, and hearing the sounds of pitches hitting the catcher's glove and bats connecting with balls—everything was more vivid that night. I would never witness a setting and atmosphere like it again in my life.

When Aaron came to the plate in the first inning, the crowd was electric, collectively ready to explode. He walked, and it was almost a letdown for fans. In the fourth inning, he came to the plate again, facing Los Angeles Dodgers pitcher Al Downing. I could feel the buzz in the crowd, and I could hear it in my own voice. As Aaron launched Downing's pitch high and long over the fence in left-center, I instinctively walked out onto the field, along with dozens of players, and by the time I hit the third-base line, Aaron was jogging toward immortality. I caught up with him just as he was crossing home plate.

"Henry, you just hit the home run!" I said with my microphone outstretched, trying to keep pace with the champ.

"Thank God it's over!" he responded as he took the final

steps to home, where he was mobbed by teammates. I just kept on recording the exchanges with his teammates, and, as they stopped the game to present Aaron with a plaque, I was in prime position to interview his parents, who had come down onto the field. I never gave one thought to breaking any media rules or having my credential revoked. I just went with the moment. Not only did I witness history, but I was part of history, with the tape recording chronicling the event and the immediate exclusive reaction from Aaron's parents and teammates.

I took a 5:30 a.m. flight back to Sarasota, and, yes, I was on the air the next morning. After my newscast, I started to receive calls from friends who had seen me at home plate. I figured it was my calling card and ticket to a big-market job.

Later that summer, at the All-Star Game in Pittsburgh, I introduced myself to Aaron and told him about the audio recording I had, including his parents.

"You're the guy in the trench coat!" Aaron recalled.

My audio recording of the game still plays in the Baseball Hall of Fame in Cooperstown, New York. Google "Craig Sager Hank Aaron" and you can watch the young twenty-something in a spotless white coat interviewing the Hall of Famer after he crossed home plate. I don't need to watch it; I was there.

13

MOVING ON UP

My work at WSPB continued, and I was on the air at twenty-four as a small-town celebrity—at least among the high school community that knew me. The package of football games had a sponsor and not only helped elevate the station in the community but actually brought in a few bucks as well. Since football was going so well, I asked Cliff if I could go out and pursue a sponsorship to do a high school basketball game of the week.

"If you can sell it, we can do it," he said.

So I immediately reached out to the schools, and we were able to assemble a great slate of games. I pounded the pavement for a sponsor and finally secured a local bank to cover the costs. Everything was in place.

But on the Wednesday before our first Friday night broadcast, Cliff came to me and told me we weren't going to do the games. He said that, while there was a marketable interest in Florida high school football on local radio, he doubted that high school basketball had the same interest, and he thought it would be a ratings disaster. Of course, that was something he could have shared with me long before. After a brief exchange in which I received few satisfactory answers from my boss, I erupted. I moved toward Cliff, grabbed him by the shirt, and lifted him against the wall. (He was a rather small guy.) I cocked my right hand and . . . stopped. I dropped my hands, turned around, and walked right out of the station.

I didn't know what to do—and really didn't understand what I had just done. I drove to the beach in Sarasota and sat on the sand, staring into the ocean, hoping the answer would come to me. I called my father and asked for advice. Not surprisingly, he ripped me for potentially ruining my career, but after some time he calmed down and persuaded me to figure it out. I did.

No, I did not apologize. Instead I got back into my car and drove to WYND, our rival station across town, and offered the basketball package and myself to the station manager.

Cliff didn't press charges, and I got myself a new job. It was a win-win for me.

After another six months on the radio in Sarasota, I decided that it was time to take another step closer to being a television sports anchor, which meant getting on television in any way possible. A buddy of mine, Wayne "Duke" Schifferly, got hold of a camera, and we went to a taping of *Superstars*, a made-for-TV competition on ABC featuring top athletes from all across the sports spectrum, so I could record some fake stand-ups for a résumé reel, wearing some very fanciful outfits. *Superstars* included professional soccer player Kyle Rote, Jr., routinely defeating more famous names from conventional sports, boxer Joe Frazier nearly drowning in the swimming competition, and O. J. Simpson outsprinting all comers in the challenges. Ironically, "Duke" saw the opportunity to double down, and, along with running camera, he went on to become O. J.'s personal bodyguard.

I spent the next several months sending out résumé tapes to television stations all over the country for a variety of on-air jobs in news, sports, and weather. My mailbox quickly filled up with rejection letters, some going so far as to let me know that I would never be on television. I kept every single letter, not so much as an incentive to become better at my craft but as a reminder of those who doubted me. Here are some of the quotes from the letters:

> *"You don't have what we are looking for."*
> *"There are no openings that meet your qualifications."*
> *"I suggest you pursue another line of work."*
> *"Don't call us, we'll call you."*
> *"We've returned your resume tape."*

There was one letter of encouragement, though, that I also kept. It was from a sportscaster in Dallas who went on to reach national fame.

> *You appear to have a lot of passion and love for your work, and I will be happy to discuss my thoughts on your resume tape with ideas on how to improve. Give me a call.*
> *Verne Lundquist*

In 1975, ABC Sports decided to add sideline reporters to its college football telecasts, and though I had little television experience at the time, I went for it. I made it down to the final five. They ended up hiring Jim Lampley, who would go on to broadcast the Olympics, boxing, football, and every other sport imaginable, and Don McGuire, who would go on to become my boss at Turner Sports from 1987 to 1995. But I didn't pick up my bat and glove and head home. I kept going after it.

After getting rejected from every station, I got a call from WLCY in Tampa/St. Petersburg, offering me a chance to audition for a meteorologist position. The first thing I did was go to a local thrift shop in Sarasota, a city dominated by retirees, and pick out a seersucker suit in yellow, blue, and white. The second thing I did was buy the *Golden Guide to Weather* and memorize meteorological terms like "cumulus clouds," "cold front," and "barometric pressure."

The good news? I nailed the audition and got the job. The bad news? The station manager told me that I had to tone down the clothes, because the camera couldn't focus when I lifted my arms to point to the map.

Weather reports should be fun, and my broadcasts tried to convey that message at least in part through my wardrobe of colorful jackets, shirts, and ties. I had fun for a while, but I quickly became bored with doing the same South Florida weather every night at 6:00 p.m. and 11:00 p.m.—other than during hurricane season, the conditions didn't exactly change. So I started to look for something else. Though my dad encouraged me to get on the news side, every ounce of my being missed the competitive world of sports and the dramatic moments it produced.

WINK-TV in Fort Myers was looking for a sports director and sports anchor, and I was in. When I left the station in Tampa, one of the requirements for my replacement, according to the station manager, was for that person to change his or her name to Sunny Day.

When I first started at WINK-TV, I was happily a one-man band. I made phone calls, lugged the camera and tripod everywhere, hit record, did interviews, edited stories, wrote scripts, and delivered sportscasts during the newscasts. I brought with me to Fort Myers my grassroots approach and work ethic, hitting as many high school games on the schedule as possible and often not getting back to the station until ten minutes before air. I also did play-by-play of local high school games, and games at nearby Edison Community College, as well as hosting pep rallies at local schools. I had never worked so hard in my life, but I loved every minute of it.

The Kansas City Royals held their spring training in Fort Myers every February and March, and WINK would regularly cover the team and its games, so I got to know many folks within the organization, including manager Whitey Herzog. When the Royals' home television station, KMBC in Kansas City, was looking for a new sports anchor and Royals pre- and postgame host in 1978, I was a finalist, but I lost out to another young broadcaster.

But in 1979, that same job opened up again, and Whitey suggested that they consider me. I got the job and made the decision to leave the sun of Florida for the flatlands of the Midwest. Kansas City was a bigger market than Fort Myers, and that's how anchors and reporters moved up in television: by moving to progressively bigger markets. In Kansas City, in addition to hosting the Royals shows and anchoring sports on the evening news, I did play-by-play for the NBA's Kansas City Kings and preseason games for the NFL's Kansas City Chiefs.

In the fall of 1980, CNN, which had made its cable debut on June 1 of that year, designated the Kansas City Royals–New York Yankees playoff series as its first sports remote, meaning that reporters would be covering the event on-site. However, Major League Baseball rejected its credential request, telling founder Ted Turner that CNN was not an accredited network and never would be. Not one to take no for an answer, Ted

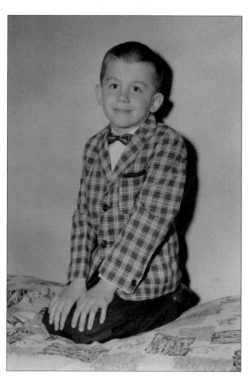

Craig as a youngster in 1958, already displaying a taste for fashion at home in Batavia.

Seven-year-old Craig in his Wyatt Earp costume, which he insisted on wearing to school every day.

After winning a local hitting contest as an eleven-year-old, Craig meets Cubs players Sammy Taylor, Frank Thomas, and his idol, Ernie Banks, in Oak Park, Illinois.

Craig (#32, *second row, standing, fourth from left*) after another district tournament basketball title at Batavia High School in 1969, with teammates, best friend John "Hondo" Clark (#24, *second row, standing, far right*), and friend Greg Issel (#42, *first row, sitting, far left*). (Courtesy of *Aurora Beacon News*)

With his parents, Coral and Al, in front of his 1935 Rolls-Royce Bentley in Sarasota in 1976.

Coral and Al Sager visiting the WINK-TV studio in 1976.

On the freshman basketball team at Northwestern in fall 1969, wearing #21.

Having some fun in the spring of 1971 as a sophomore at Northwestern with friend and fraternity brother Rich Rushkewicz.

Craig as Willie the Wildcat before a Northwestern football game in 1972.

Craig was a one-man band at WINK-TV in Fort Myers in the mid-1970s.

In a colorful suit Craig bought at a thrift store in Sarasota for his meteorologist audition, presiding at a banquet in Fort Myers in 1974. (Courtesy of Gene Marderness Photography)

As Hank Aaron prepares to cross home plate after his historic home run in Atlanta in 1974, Craig, in an all-white suit, is ready to meet him. (Courtesy of Tony Triolo / *Sports Illustrated Classic*)

Craig, a radio reporter in Sarasota, joins in the media scrum around tennis Hall of Famer Billie Jean King in 1974.

Craig sits with Cincinnati Reds' star Pete Rose in the spring-training dugout in 1976.

Hosting *Inside the NBA* in 1991 along with a future partner, Craig II, age two. (Courtesy of Turner Sports)

With the boxing legend Muhammad Ali and Craig II in Atlanta in 1993.

Ryan, age eight, with NBA All-Star LeBron James.

Before the deluge of the bulls in Pamplona, 2001.

Stacy and Craig in Australia after the Goodwill Games in 2001.

Craig with Charles Barkley at the 27th Annual Sports Emmy Awards in New York. (Courtesy of Marc Bryan-Brown / Getty Images Sport)

The Sager family in April 2016. Sitting, from left: Ryan, Craig, Stacy, and Riley. Standing, from left: Krista, Craig II, and Kacy. (Photo courtesy of Cancer Care)

Craig with Dr. Naveen Pemmaraju at MD Anderson Cancer Center in Houston in 2016. (Photo courtesy of KHOU-TV)

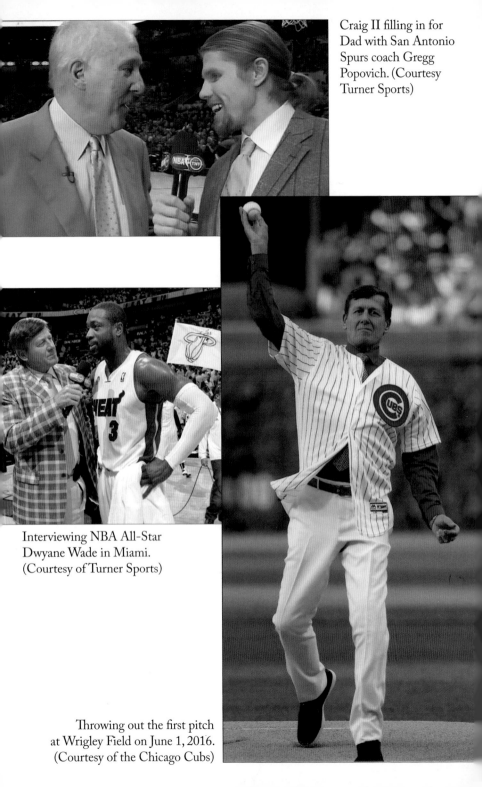

Craig II filling in for Dad with San Antonio Spurs coach Gregg Popovich. (Courtesy Turner Sports)

Interviewing NBA All-Star Dwyane Wade in Miami. (Courtesy of Turner Sports)

Throwing out the first pitch at Wrigley Field on June 1, 2016. (Courtesy of the Chicago Cubs) called Royals public relations director Dean Vogelaar, looking for ideas to bail out CNN. Dean told him to call me, as I would be covering the series, and it just so happened that I lived with two of the Royals' players—Craig Chamberlain and Steve Mingori—along with PR assistant Mike Swanson.

After speaking with Ted, I agreed to record my story segments to air on KMBC in Kansas City and then record a different tag line or ending and turn it over to the guys at CNN to air. Nobody watched the channel at the time, so I was never concerned that my bosses would see it.

Flash-forward five months to March 1981, when I received a call from CNN asking if I would come take a tour of their Atlanta headquarters. On a layover in Atlanta, en route to do a Royals spring training game, I visited with Ted Turner, and he promised me an hour each night devoted to sports, which was a hell of a lot better than the three minutes I was doing on the newscasts. And that's how I became CNN employee number 343.

Being part of a start-up network was at once frustrating and invigorating. In those early years, we had little credibility and limited resources, but even as we tried to find our sea legs, we produced some great television. As CNN expanded, along with its sister network, TBS, we were able to create college football and basketball programming, cover the Goodwill Games, and report from around the world. When we landed the NBA contract in 1984, it was a game changer. Michael Jordan and the NBA were exploding, and in 1988 came the launch of TNT, the current home of the NBA. Turner Broadcasting shelled out a whopping $20 million to secure the rights to NBA games in a two-year deal in 1984, which at the time seemed astronomical to rights holders. But with the arrival of a new generation of superstars, the NBA was taking off. Four years later, the deal was worth $50 million. (For comparison's sake, the contract today costs Turner a reported $1.2 billion a year.)

I have been with Turner ever since, covering every sport imaginable on almost every continent. I have witnessed some amazing events, but more important, I have experienced the emotions that sports bring out. One of those moments was in New York City in 2001.

Like most Americans, I remember where I was when I first learned of the September 11 attacks, and I couldn't have been farther away from New York. I had just wrapped up my broadcasting duties with Turner at the Goodwill Games in Brisbane, Australia. Stacy had come with me on the trip, and our return flight to the States was on Tuesday, September 11, though most of the Turner crew had flown out on Monday. On Monday evening (Tuesday morning in New York), we were out to dinner when video of the planes crashing into the World Trade Center started to replay on the televisions at the restaurant. Trite to say it, but it was surreal. I immediately thought of my father and called him, and Dad was in full fighting mode.

"We got to go to war with them," he insisted, ready to enlist even in his eighties.

Not unexpectedly, with the American airports shut down, our flight was canceled.

I made it to New York early on September 21, in time for the Mets–Braves game, which was being broadcast on TBS. Major League Baseball had put its schedule on hold immediately following the attacks, and this was the first game in New York City after the attacks. I knew it would be an emotional game for all involved, and the stands were packed with first responders, many of whom had spent the past ten days searching for survivors—and then bodies—at Ground Zero. The pregame tribute to the victims was emotional, as was the national anthem. For a good part of the telecast, I reported from the left-center-field section, where many New York City firefighters fought back tears. The game of baseball was clearly just a respite—a distraction—if only for a few hours. When the Mets' Mike Piazza hit a mammoth two-run home run in the bottom of the eighth inning to put the Mets ahead, 3–2, the 41,235 in attendance erupted into not only a cheer I hadn't heard all game, but one I'd never heard in my baseball-going career. I interviewed Mayor Rudy Giuliani during the game and Piazza after the game. Those interviews just felt so different from any others I'd ever done.

While in New York, I was given a tour of Ground Zero. As it is for anyone who spent time there, particularly in the first few weeks post-9/11, it is hard to describe the sensations and the feelings. A layer of smoke hovered over the area, and the smell from fires permeated the scene.

It was shortly after my visit to New York that I donated my frequent flier miles to the NYC Fire Department, because those men and women needed free trips more than I did.

I will never forget those days in New York, just as the Hank Aaron home run game is etched in my memory.

14

VICTORY

In late April 2014, I was a week into my chemotherapy treatment at Northside Hospital, and so far, I felt no ill effects from the chemo. *This isn't so bad*, I remember thinking. The game plan that Dr. Holland had set up was to first kill all the existing evidence of leukemia in my body—the "blasts"—and then get me into remission, meaning with little or no evidence of any blasts.

A strong measure of the stage of the disease is the amount of blasts in the bloodstream. If abnormal immature white blood cells fill the bone marrow and flush into the bloodstream, it causes an array of serious issues, including limiting the production of healthy blood cells. For healthy humans, the percentage of blasts in the blood at any given time is zero. My blood contained 27 percent when I was first diagnosed.

If I could get into remission, we could consider doing a stem cell transplant, which is really the only hope for an AML patient. Rarely will the leukemia go away with just chemo and never return. So it's best if a donor can be found, so that their stem cells can help create a new, healthy way for the patient's body to produce blood cells.

While we waited to see if the chemo had an effect on the blasts, which could take two to three weeks, doctors were already in the process of identifying a potential match for a transplant. In fact, as soon as I was admitted to the hospital, doctors had begun the often lengthy process of identifying any potential matches in Europe, as it has the largest blood donor base in the world. But even if doctors could find a match in Europe, professionals would then need to find the anonymous donor, get his or her agreement to move forward with the process, collect the needed marrow, and ship it to the States. This search could take months, so the doctors turned to my family for help in finding a donor as I continued to receive treatment.

Meanwhile, day after day, there was routine testing of my vitals and of my blood, and the occasional painful bone marrow biopsy. I felt strong as the days wore on, and my blood levels seemed to indicate that I was responding well to the chemo. On May 10 (day nineteen of my being in the Blood and Marrow Transplant unit), Dr. Holland came in the room during his rounds.

"You can go," he said, as matter-of-factly as you can deliver surprisingly great news.

"I can go?" I asked incredulously. *"Today?"*

"Yes, Craig," he said, smiling. "You can go home today. You still need to come in every day for treatment and testing, but you can go home."

I almost jumped out of the hospital bed, pulled out my IV, and gave the man a hug. *Thirty days* in the hospital? Not me. He explained that the blasts in my bloodstream were decreasing every day. He also said that he and his colleagues were amazed at how well my body had responded to the chemo.

Of course, going home came with restrictions. I was told to avoid mowing the lawn, taking out the trash, picking up the dog poop, or doing any household maintenance—to which Stacy replied, "That shouldn't be a problem. He doesn't do those things anyway."

When we got home, Riley came out to the driveway before I even got out of the car and gave me a huge hug. Ryan was at a friend's birthday party, and Stacy decided that we would surprise him when he returned. I came into the house after being away for almost three weeks, and I felt great. We laughed a little, I ate some food, and then I went upstairs to lie down in my own bed.

When Ryan came home, Stacy was waiting.

"I have a surprise for you," she told him through a few tears. "Go look in Mommy's bedroom."

He walked into the room and immediately sprinted the ten steps to the bed and leaned over and gave me a hug.

"I can't believe it!" he said excitedly. "You're home! Now I don't have to imagine you in my dreams anymore." My heart melted.

The next day, I was right back at Northside Hospital, where Stacy and I would go every morning for the next few months after taking the kids to school, spending six or seven hours a day there in the early days, having transfusions and getting platelet refueling. Five days after Dr. Holland had released me, he announced that I was in complete remission. The chemo had worked! I had beaten AML. I had not been so excited in weeks. I couldn't wait to get back to work and onto the golf course.

But remission was just the first step, I remembered. I still needed the transplant, and Dr. Holland targeted early July for the procedure. He also told me that I needed another five days of chemo, starting June 2, to make sure that there were no signs of leukemia in my body as we headed toward the transplant, although he did concede that I could get the chemo as an out-patient.

But I still needed a donor match. And wouldn't you know it: the match was Craig Sager.

15

A Match

My siblings and I were told that finding a donor to give Dad
a bone marrow transplant was the only option for long-term
remission. The online research I had been doing since his
diagnosis prepared me for the possibility of a transplant.
Hearing it for the first time, however, was something
I wasn't quite prepared for.

To me, bone marrow was that yellowish, spongy stuff
in the middle of bones that I had no appetite for visualizing.
Now it had become the only way to save my dad's life. I
could envision them extracting it out of his body. I could
picture all the new cells that would have to fill his hollow
bones to build an entire new immune system from scratch.
My dad was going to have to go through this dangerous
procedure, and I fully grasped how complicated, terrifying,
and incredible this process was going to be.

After hearing that a transplant was the route we were
taking, I soon became convinced that I was going to
be the one to donate the bone marrow, even though the

statistics weren't in my favor. Finding a match is a long shot—there are six leukocyte antigen key markers that the tests compare between the donor and the recipient, and the doctors suggested that there was only a 25 percent chance that I would match on half. The odds of being the perfect donor they were searching for were even lower— only 2 percent of children share all six markers with a parent—but no matter how long it had been or what age I was at, spending father-son time always reminded me of just how much the two of us are alike. We had the same competitive drive, the same constant craving for excitement, and the same behaviors and mannerisms—even the same taste in clothes. Everything I felt inside myself when I was in my own world was in him, too, I believed, only amplified.

The donor testing process can be done with a swift cotton swab of the mouth to collect a DNA sample, but for family members, nurses go straight to blood tests to accelerate the steps. My biggest obstacle was getting over my fear of needles. As a kid, if I knew I had a doctor's appointment in a month, that whole month was ruined. One of the happiest days of my childhood was when I talked a doctor out of giving me a finger prick.

When my sisters and I, along with my Aunt Candy, got tested at Northside Hospital on May 6, the second the blood started to come out, I felt myself getting ready to pass out—an uncontrollable response. My vision was the first to go, followed by the irritation and pain of pins and needles all over my body. I started to sway, and then *boom!* The next thing I know, I'm coming to with the help of the nurses. Somehow, before I passed out, they had collected enough blood in the vial.

On May 22, Dad called to tell me that I was a perfect

six for six on the original indicators, and further testing
had shown that I was a ten for ten, or, in the transplant
world, "a perfect match." It was confirmation of what
I had always known—that we were even more deeply
connected than our names.

"When are we doing this thing?" I said, clapping my
hands together. We were looking at early July for the date
of the bone marrow transplant. I knew what the timing
meant: that my family's tradition of running the Peachtree
Road Race in Atlanta every Fourth of July was in
jeopardy.

Dad hadn't missed a race in thirty years. I had run it at
his side the past nine, and had been training for six
months to improve my time. No matter how busy we
were, we always had the Fourth of July off, and I could
count on my dad being at the finish line, ready to throw
down a couple of ice-cold 8:00 a.m. beers with me. The
thought of our first beer at the finish line shaved minutes
off my time every year. It was hard enough knowing he
wasn't going to be running it with us this year, but if *I*
couldn't do it, either? I had already purchased an extra bib
number to run with, in his honor, to make sure the whole
family still had our annual matching Peachtree Road Race
finishers' T-shirt.

While I was in San Antonio covering Game Three of
the NBA Finals for work, my dad called. "I'm sorry,
Junior," he said. "July third. That's the date. I tried, but I
won't be ready anytime sooner."

"Don't you worry," I responded. "I am running that
race no matter what."

I returned from my trip to the Finals for a day of
pre-transplant prep work on June 11. Six hours, eighteen

vials, and two bags of blood later, I finally walked out of the hospital. I couldn't believe I had made it through all of that without passing out this time. But I also realized that if I couldn't donate blood, I was going to be screwed trying to donate bone marrow.

The next three weeks leading up to the transplant were eye-opening for me. I knew I wasn't the first person to donate bone marrow, but this was my father. I was able to see both perspectives of the transplant on a deeply personal level. I saw him undergo the chemotherapy and radiation that killed him from the inside out so he could be reborn and grow a new immune system. It is an overpowering emotional medley with nothing else I could possibly compare it to. Love, fear, hope, and excitement all blended together in an actual life-or-death situation.

On July 2, the eve of the transplant, I visited him in his room. Dad had been admitted five days earlier for some precautionary chemotherapy and antibiotics. The first thing we did was our own version of the Peachtree Road Race. We walked twelve laps around the isolation floor, which amounted to a full mile, and then went back to his room so he could detail the day ahead of us. My check-in was at 6:00 a.m., and he was going to receive the bone marrow once they retrieved it from my room, two buildings and seven floors away.

When I got home that night after our visit, I opened a handwritten note that my father had penned and given to me at the hospital:

Dear Craig II,
I want to be like you, you want to be like me, and now we're going to become "blood brothers"—explain that one!

*You've always made me proud, but there is no way to put in
words your miraculous gift that will save my life.*
Well done my son, well done!

Transplant day was tense. I didn't get to see my dad
that morning before I was wheeled back for the harvest.
I'd had four football-related surgeries in my lifetime, but
those were all to fix something. This time I was perfectly
healthy. It was strange to know I was about to get bone
marrow sucked out of my body while being out cold, but I
was relieved to finally be getting this day over with.

An hour and a half later, I woke up in a waiting room.
They had drilled a hole into each of my hips, just above
where the pockets would be on the back of a pair of jeans,
to extract the marrow. I had a thick pad pressed into my
hips and up to my lower back, locked in place with a
corset of cohesive bandage tape. In all, doctors had
extracted 1.5 liters of liquid bone marrow, which was a lot.

To say I was uncomfortable was an understatement. I
was lying down on my back, which had two holes in it.
Shifting slightly in any direction pressed the bulky pad-
ding right into what felt like a deep bone bruise. I couldn't
move. While I recovered, they detected premature ven-
tricular contractions—abnormal heartbeats that began in
one of the heart's two lower pumping chambers. I was
held in the recovery room for two hours while I begged
them to at least let me call my dad and family to let them
know that I was okay. Other patients in the recovery room
were groggy and fighting off the wake-up attempts by the
nurses, but I couldn't have been more wide-awake. I was
ready to get the hell out of there.

I was taken to a separate part of the hospital for further

testing with a cardiologist who told me that I was going to have to stay overnight until my 11 a.m. post-op blood tests the next day, because they were concerned about my heartbeat. Word had been passed on to the doctor that I was going to try to run the race on July 4, and he was not going to let me risk it. A visit from Patient Relations, the head of cardiology, and the lead doctor of the transplant led to my eventual release, on the stipulation that I would not run in the race.

They wheeled me out of the hospital at 5:00 p.m.—the exact same moment my dad was walking out to the parking lot. It felt like the universe had aligned to give us this moment. I hadn't even considered the possibility that he might be able to go home that day. All the delays and all the struggling to get out of the hospital led to a perfectly timed discharge. We were standing in the parking lot, enjoying the fresh air together, free from the hospital's walls. He had a birthday cake hat on his head, to commemorate his "first day of birth" with my DNA. A lifetime of being shown how to enjoy the moment couldn't describe what I felt seeing him outside of the hospital walls once again. The air felt fresher, the world looked brighter, and all the things we'd be able to do once he was fully recovered filled me with an endless supply of hope.

I had two holes in my hip bone, with no painkillers. I had no energy, because of my depleted bone marrow and a massive anesthesia hangover. None of that mattered as I crossed the finish line of the Peachtree Road Race. Against all advice, medically and parentally, I completed the 10K in 1:18 that next morning. It was obviously brutal.

In addition to the race, I had to walk two miles just to get to the starting line. I couldn't stand up straight because of the bandage that was locked in place for someone who was not meant to be moving at all. I ran a 6.2-mile race with the thick bandages pressing against my tender lower back every step of the way. I was hunched over the whole time, which hurt my back even more. But I made it. My dad had my bone marrow in him, but I showed him that I have his spirit in me.

16

A NEW BIRTHDAY

The transplant procedure day was not much different from a typical day for me in the hospital. The doctor came in with a nurse, who wheeled in some equipment and a portable X-ray machine. They connected an IV tube to my catheter and, after a first burst of cold in my veins, it felt like a typical transfusion or chemo as my son's stem cells poured into my body. I had O positive blood, and Junior had A positive, so if the transplant was successful, in two to three weeks, my blood would turn to A positive, producing healthy blood cells and hopefully keeping leukemia out of my body forever.

True to its word, Northside discharged me that very same afternoon and, as Junior says, we ran into each other in the parking lot. The thrill of going home was soon diminished when Dr. Holland called a few hours later to let me know that the lab had detected *C. diff* in my stool, a possibly life-threatening infection in my situation, for which they prescribed some antibiotics to fight off the infection.

The rounds of chemo over the past few months had wiped

out my immune system, and I was very susceptible to the tiniest of infections—many of which could lead to death. We were instructed to take all kinds of precautions at home. Among the prohibited activities for six months post-transplant: no working in an office, no movie theaters, no sporting events, no animals, no lawn work, no swimming, no alcohol, no visitors outside of family, and no restaurants. Even hugging my kids was risky, as children are often carriers of multiple germs. Despite all of the restrictions, I couldn't wait to be back home.

Riley and Ryan were waiting with WELCOME HOME! signs and arms outstretched for hugs as we pulled into the driveway. With the transplant behind me, and my family in front of me, I felt renewed.

For the next week, I grew accustomed to a routine at home: watching television, spending time with the kids and Stacy, and, when I was up for it, riding the exercise bike in the basement to rebuild my strength. The antibiotics seemed to be working on the *C. diff*, and I was feeling better each day. On July 12, however, I came down with a fever, and Stacy was under strict instructions to get me back to the hospital for any temperature above 100.5. We raced to Northside and I was back in an isolation room. Within a day, doctors had diagnosed pneumonia in my lungs, which can be fatal in a transplant patient.

The most critical days after a transplant are the first nineteen to twenty-one days, while the donor blood and stem cells overtake the patient's. When patients hit day one hundred after transplant, doctors feel comfortable that the transplant was successful. I was still medicated up: tramadol, Colace, hydrocortisone, NeutraSal, Uloric, Actigall, Pepcid, Klor-Con, acyclovir, Flomax, and dozens more. Some I took multiple times a day, some once a day, and some only as needed. My pillboxes looked like a Rite-Aid store shelf, and the medications changed daily or weekly depending on what the doctors ordered.

I tried to remain upbeat, but these were difficult days. Every time I seemed to have won a battle, something would pull me back down. I never thought of giving up, but admittedly, I was sad and frustrated. After a few more days in the hospital, fighting off the pneumonia, doctors thought I was well enough to return home, but a few days later I was right back at Northside, with a high fever caused by the pneumonia that I thought I had just beaten. This time, I wouldn't be going anywhere for a while.

Doctors conducted two bronchoscopies and multiple CT scans to determine whether the round mass detected in my lung, caused by the pneumonia, was viral or fungal. They put me on eight strong antibiotics to cover the bases, though they never came to a conclusion. In addition to the pneumonia, my feet had swelled and turned purple—I had developed a serious case of gout in my feet, making it very painful to take even one step. But as an active man and avid runner, I couldn't just lie in bed all day. I got an old man's walker and took a few steps in the hospital ward. I wasn't embarrassed by using the walker; I was just thrilled to be moving. I was, however, upset that the nurses insisted that someone must walk next to me in case I lost my balance and fell. I started out with one lap on the first day, then three laps the following day, then four laps, then six laps three times a day. Despite all this, I loved my walks.

My stay in the hospital was longer than anyone had expected. July turned into August, August into September, September into October. Stacy gave me daily companionship while Mary Jo, my seventy-nine-year-old mother-in-law, who defies her age and who had moved to Atlanta from Chicago, helped care for

Riley and Ryan and our eighty-pound boxer, Princess Jasmine. Because the kids were too young to visit me in my room, on special occasions, Mary Jo and the kids would appear on the yard outside of my fourth-floor hospital room blowing kisses, holding signs, and waving. Although the windows on the floor did not open, a safeguard against outside germs getting in, the sight of Riley and Ryan was like a breath of fresh air, reminding me that I was not imprisoned, that this confinement was temporary.

I spent ninety-three straight days in the hospital before doctors thought I was well enough to continue my recovery at home. I said my goodbyes to the nurses and fellow patients on the floor as they wheeled me to the main entrance, to where Stacy had pulled the car around. I could feel the rays of sunshine hit every inch of my body, I could smell the flowers from many feet away, I could hear the chirps of birds, and I began to cry as I slowly got up out of the wheelchair and took the final few steps on my own.

I spent my days at home going back and forth with Stacy to the clinic or sitting on the sofa watching television. For a guy who has been on the move his entire life, I had to change my lifestyle dramatically. The hospital walls and my own house felt like a prison at times, though just being out of the hospital was a relief. I fought back the forces of depression by focusing on tomorrow and by unequivocally believing that not only would I make it back to the NBA sidelines but that I would beat leukemia altogether. I had lost fifty-seven pounds and, frankly, was grateful just to be alive.

There was a positive side to my confinement, of course: I got to spend a lot of time with my children and my bride. Keep in mind, I had rarely been in the same city for more than a week or two since I'd married Stacy, and certainly since we had Riley and Ryan, so we all adjusted to being together. I snuck out to the golf course and tried to hit some balls—swinging and missing three straight times my first time out—and putted on the greens with Ryan. I watched my kids practice and play tennis, seated courtside with my mask, and I occasionally broke the rules about not driving and made quick trips to the McDonald's drive-thru to grab a double cheeseburger with no onions or a grilled Filet-O-Fish sandwich with no lettuce.

Doctors typically tell transplant patients that they can't return to work for twelve to eighteen months after the procedure. Although I really wanted to be back on the NBA sidelines for the opening of the season in late October, I came to accept the fact that it would not happen, so I set my sights on another goal: the 2015 NBA All-Star Game in New York City, in mid-February. Sure, it was still well before most patients are given the green light to travel and return to work, but maybe I could rewrite the rules a bit.

In October, I received a one-hundred-day certificate from the transplant nurses at Northside:

CONGRATULATIONS

CRAIG SAGER

ON REACHING THIS MILESTONE
WITH YOUR TRANSPLANT THERAPY

I have been honored to receive awards and certificates throughout my life for various accomplishments, but at the time this one meant more than all the others. Despite the dark days, the setbacks, the *C. diff*, the pneumonia, I had made it one hundred days post-transplant, and doctors were optimistic it was working. Junior had literally and figuratively saved my life.

One of the greatest threats to a transplant recipient is the appearance of graft-versus-host disease (GVHD). In plain terms, this is when the stem cells from the donor (or graft) form a new immune system in the recipient but the new system recognizes the recipient (host) as being different and, instead of protecting the body, attacks it. GVHD can be fatal. I was fortunate that there was no evidence of GVHD in my body. However, doctors put me on Prograft, an immunosuppressant, for six months to avoid GVHD, which meant that any travel was too risky for my immune system. The six-month period would end March 1, 2015, two weeks *after* the All-Star Game in New York City.

By late January, after regular treatments at Northside, I had gained some weight back, my hair had returned, and my gout was gone, as was my pneumonia.

The transplant had taken hold, although there were some concerning signs in my blood, as my white blood cell numbers were trending down, though doctors believed that it could just be a side effect of the Prograft. Nevertheless, I was ready to return to work.

17

"I'M BACK, BABY!"

I met with Dr. Holland on January 31, and we discussed my return to the airwaves. Well, it really wasn't much of a discussion. Dr. Holland, concerned about my frail immune system, did not want me to go to New York for the All-Star Game. When I pushed back, he suggested that I could drive to New York or take a private plane, to avoid the germ-infested airports. However, when he also stipulated that I could not shake any hands, give any hugs, or have any human physical contact, I decided it wasn't worth it.

Though my goal of the All-Star Game didn't happen, TNT did arrange for me to interview Carmelo Anthony over satellite during All-Star Weekend—me from Orlando, where Dr. Holland had allowed us to drive, and Carmelo from outside the locker room in New York before tip-off—so I could continue my streak of being a part of one of my favorite weekends of the year.

In March, doctors finally cleared me to travel, and I marked Chicago for my first game back, on March 5. I had not been on-air since the game in Dallas in April 2014, before my diagnosis, and I was a bit nervous about being back on the sidelines. I wanted Stacy with me, so we flew out a few days before so I could get acclimated, go to the shootarounds, and otherwise find my footing. The night before the game, Stacy and I had a quick bite to eat and came back to the hotel, a deviation from my regular routine of staying out late with friends or the Turner crew at a local watering hole. But that night was different, and I understood that rest was critical.

Unbeknownst to me, Mike Bartlett, Chris Chattin, Mike Joehl, Ricky Haynes, Dave Pasterz, Tony Sarallo, Barry White, and Steve Zahorodny, eight of my golfing buddies from Georgia, had flown in for the game, and many friends from Batavia drove over as well. I put on my ensemble and made my way over to the United Center. My phone was blowing up with supportive texts:

WELCOME BACK my friend. The NBA is not the same without the INCOMPARABLE SAGS!!! The BEST TEAMMATE EVER!!!
—Doug Collins, former NBA head coach and Turner broadcaster

Craig, I heard you are back to work tonight! I can't tell you how happy that makes all of us in Cleveland and as well as me personally. There has been "something missing" since you left to fight your medical challenge. Welcome back and stay back!
—Dan Gilbert, owner, Cleveland Cavaliers

It was an odd feeling being back. The outpouring of love and support from fans, players, and coaches was truly overwhelming, but as much as I appreciated the gestures, I really just wanted things to be normal. Normal meant talking about basketball, gathering some information, and reporting on the game.

The Bulls did a nice video tribute in my honor, and the standing ovation from the United Center crowd almost brought me to tears as I thought about all that I had been through to get back to this place.

The next morning, Stacy and I flew back to Atlanta, as I had previously scheduled labs at Northside Hospital. I was preparing to go on the road for a few weeks to cover the NCAA Tournament, and the doctors wanted one last check-in before my long trip.

I was in such a great mood that I didn't even mind suffering through yet another bone marrow biopsy and an array of blood tests. It was actually good to see some familiar faces, which again gave me perspective on just how far I had come.

One of my favorite nurses, Janet Benn, was a forty-something barrel of laughs and energy. We would talk golf courses and basketball, and she admitted that she had been a big fan of mine for years. One reason she was a favorite was that she was the only one at Northside who performed a bone marrow biopsy on me that didn't send me into delirious screams.

So when Janet walked into the room a few hours after the biopsy and blood tests, I was buoyed by her presence.

"So what's the good news?" I asked.

Her eyes told me all I needed to know.

Dr. Holland came in shortly after to let me know that I was no longer in remission. And it was bad. It wasn't just that the leukemia had returned but that it had returned with a vengeance.

"Three to four weeks," he said.

How would you react if someone told you that you had three to four weeks left on this earth?

I had no choice but to simply decide right then and there that I was not going to die in three weeks. I never gave the matter much consideration. I had too much to live for. I was not going to let the leukemia win.

When Stacy broke down in tears, it broke my heart. We were both emotional that day, one of the worst days of my life. It was actually a wake-up call to me. I finally realized, after almost a year, that leukemia would not be defeated easily and could eventually kill me—but, I decided, not anytime soon. After I went into remission in 2014 and had the successful transplant in July, I had figured I was home free. But after all that, plus the chemo, the pneumonia, the gout, the pain, here I was again. My fight was not over.

Dr. Holland put me on a ten-day round of chemo, which failed to make much of a difference. My pneumonia came back strong, and I was hospitalized again in late March and stayed for a few weeks. My condition was worsening, and my options for recovery were narrowing fast. After another biopsy came back with 30 percent blasts, Stacy and I were desperate and needed to try something different. We consulted with Dr. Holland and decided that we would go to MD Anderson Cancer Center in Houston, which is world-renowned for its care and for its many clinical trials, which are often last resorts for patients who are running out of treatment options.

By this time, I had already blown past the three-to-four-week death sentence from Dr. Holland by a few months, but I understood that time was critical. Funny how time takes on new meaning when others tell you that you don't have much of it left.

We went home and packed our bags for a stay at MD Anderson, and my first concern was, what was I going to wear on my first day in Houston?

18

THE COLORS OF ME

Many young children have their "thing," usually in the form of a well-worn blanket, a stuffed animal, or maybe even an unexciting piece of cloth. For me, I was obsessed with my Wyatt Earp costume. On a trip to spring training with my family when I was seven, my parents bought me a Wyatt Earp ensemble, complete with a black hat, white shirt with red stars, and black bow tie. I was thrilled to proudly wear it to a Boston Red Sox spring training game, and it made for some funny looks while I got autographs. But after Red Sox infielder Billy Consolo thought I was adorable in my Earp outfit, he took me back into the locker room, where I got all of the players' autographs, including the great Ted Williams. When I returned to school in Batavia, I wore that costume *every day* for the rest of the year. *Every day.* Maybe I thought it brought me good fortune, or perhaps it was a comfort thing for me at the time—a security blanket in an unusual way. Or maybe it was just the seed of my lifelong love of fashion.

Batavia High School was like thousands of other small high

schools in small towns in 1969—boring, conformist, and ordinary, and the senior portraits in the yearbook reflected just that. Every boy was required to wear a black or navy blazer with a white collared shirt for his senior yearbook photo, and each year, every portrait looked the same. One after the other. I wanted to mix it up, and a Monkee gave me an idea.

The Monkees were a pop quartet in the late 1960s with their own popular television show, and their initial albums created many a hit, including "Daydream Believer." Davy Jones, one of the lead singers, fashionably wore an electric-blue Nehru jacket with a white collar, a hip-length coat inspired by the former prime minister of India and a look made popular by the Beatles. I found myself a Nehru jacket in a nearby town and decided that it reflected my personality.

When I walked in for my school portrait, the photographer thought I was joking, and my classmates did not believe I would go through with it. But I argued with the photographer, and he finally relented when he recognized I was not budging and that the photo would have to be retaken anyway. He was wrong on the second part. The 1969 Batavia High School yearbook has a lot of boys wearing blazers, but not me.

At Northwestern, when I joined the cheerleading team and became the mascot, everything in my dorm room closet was purple (the school color). I was all in, and wearing bright colors—like purple—just made me feel better.

My insistence on bright, colorful outfits continued in a rather odd way once I entered the professional world. When the meteorologist job opened in Tampa, I picked out the yellow-blue-and-white seersucker suit. In Fort Myers, I jumped at every chance to wear the school colors of a host high school for pep rallies and football games. When I moved on to Kansas City, which had cold winters, the bright colors did not fly as much on-air, but I still managed to wear lively shirts and coats. After I was hired at CNN in 1981, Ted Turner told me that CNN was fighting for credibility and that I needed to tone down my look. I did my best, some days just wearing a colorful tie on-air, but as I became more entrenched at the network, I felt comfortable pushing the boundaries of my wardrobe.

But the attention on my attire really took off when I began to do sideline for NBA games on TNT in the 1980s. By then, my closet was full of hundreds of colorful shirts, suits, ties, and shoes, and I attempted to never wear the same combination twice. For the 2001 NBA All-Star Game in Washington, I picked out a dashing black-and-silver jacket with a black shirt and silver tie. I ignored some of the smirks as I got set for the broadcast, but I was devastated halfway through when my producers told me that I had to change jackets by order of the NBA commissioner and the president of the network. I felt like a part of me was being ripped away. I changed into a less shocking jacket and finished the broadcast, but I was hurt.

When Commissioner David Stern instituted a league-wide dress code for coaches and players, he expected their network partners to do the same. So when I knew the commissioner would be in attendance at a game I was covering, I always tried to tone it down. But one game, unaware that Stern and his wife, Dianne, would be in the stands, I wore a typical Sager outfit and could tell that he was giving me the once-over from his seat. I went over and shook his hand, and when his wife complimented me on my outfit, noting that "sports is fun," the commissioner seemed to change his demeanor. From then on, I never felt like I was under his microscope.

Now there is pressure for me to deliver bold outfits game

after game, city after city. The players often approach me before games to talk about my selection or to give me suggestions on tailors or designers.

My clothes reflect who I am. I believe that life should be fun and so should your clothes. It's not about attention or even sending a message; it's about feeling good about yourself and being who you are. After my diagnosis, I began to wear a lot of orange on-air once I returned to the broadcasts. Orange is the color of the leukemia awareness effort, and I even had a bright orange blazer specially made for me.

In Houston it was difficult for me to create colorful ensembles as a leukemia patient every day, but I did wear multicolored shorts or shirts to brighten the day a bit. (A good friend, Steve Koonin, had a sequined hospital gown made for me, and Marv Albert had a Superman cape tailored for me for hospital needs.) And I was thankful for these gifts, as I needed every ounce of brightness.

PART III

HOUSTON

19

DR. P

In the early twentieth century, Monroe Anderson and his partners ran the world's largest business in the cotton trade. Based in Texas, Anderson amassed enormous wealth, and with some of it, he established the MD Anderson Foundation, mostly so his heirs could avoid hefty estate taxes upon his death, which occurred in 1939. In the ensuing years, the foundation's trustees, with no specific direction from the founder on how to distribute the monies, decided to allocate $500,000 to the building of a cancer hospital in Houston, which would bear Anderson's name.

Today, MD Anderson Cancer Center is ranked the number-one cancer hospital in the world. Its more than 20,000 employees serve 135,000 patients annually, with 9,400 patients in clinical trials. Not only does MDA excel in patient care, but it is known throughout the world as the leading cancer research institution, investing almost $1 billion a year in research. It is part of the Texas Medical Center in downtown Houston, a sprawling 1,345-acre campus of twenty-one hospitals, hundreds of buildings, and an impressive record of saving—or extending—millions of lives, including those of the more than 160,000 daily visitors.

With my blasts at more than 30 percent and the chemo given to me at Northside Hospital no longer effective, Stacy and I were pinning our hopes on the professionals at MDA. Our initial appointment was scheduled for May 6, so Stacy and I flew down a day early, as I am always more comfortable when I have the lay of the land. We checked into the hotel and walked around the medical center grounds, locating the buildings for my appointments the following day. I wasn't nervous. In a way, I was excited. I had hope.

I was overwhelmed when we walked through the main entrance on the 6th—by the size of the building, the number of patients, and the schedule handed to us upon check-in. There were dozens of appointments scheduled over the next few days, on all floors of multiple buildings. Blood tests on one floor; scans on another; consultations on yet another. Everywhere we went, there were cancer patients, in various visible stages of their fight.

Number 1144411. Those digits are now me. It is my identity within the hospital walls. It is unique to me, of course, but also a reminder that I am just one of thousands who come to MD Anderson seeking help.

After an exhausting day as a guinea pig, we finally met with my assigned doctor, Naveen Pemmaraju. I didn't know what to expect from yet another doctor, but I know I was expecting a miracle. It was clear from just a few minutes with "Dr. P" that we had come to the right place. Dr. P is a brilliant hematologist, oncologist, and leukemia specialist with a witty, compassionate, effervescent personality who would just as soon discuss Kobe Bryant's retirement, Tiger Woods's slump, and Michael Jordan's drive as he would the mechanics of platelet dysfunction, the specifics of leukemia cell kill, and the inner workings of clinical trials. After reviewing my medical history with me, Dr. Pemmaraju was candid in his assessment but also optimistic about our game plan: to get me into a clinical trial and get me healthy. I liked his brand of positivity.

Clinical trials are the saving grace for thousands of cancer patients around the world. A clinical trial allows doctors to offer early-stage drugs to patients before they have been approved by the FDA, although just getting permission for a clinical trial to begin can take up to two years.

Patients, desperately in need of new treatments, benefit, of course, if the drug works. The doctors benefit, as their research helps determine the success rate of drugs on various strata of patients. The drug manufacturers benefit by using clinical trials to test the effectiveness of their drugs, which helps them gain approval from the FDA—which enables them to make billions.

Trials are divided into four phases, each with varying sizes of pools and goals, depending on the rarity of a particular cancer. Phase I allows doctors to find a safe dosage of a drug for patients, who typically number between fifteen and thirty, to determine how a new treatment should be given and to monitor its effects on the body. Phase II has fewer than one hundred patients and focuses on the effects of the new treatment on certain cancers and the body. Phase III can have from a hundred up to thousands of patients, and doctors use Phase III to compare a new treatment with the current standard treatment. Finally, Phase IV looks at a large group to study long-term safety and effectiveness.

A clinical trial was likely my only hope, but first I needed chemo—and fast. Dr. Pemmaraju came up with a plan. Nurses showed me the isolation unit where they planned for me to stay, but there was no way I was doing isolation again, despite the risks—especially after they told me that even Stacy couldn't come into the room. I would have died from a broken heart before leukemia got to me.

When I was finally admitted on May 14, my blast count was 34 percent and rising, and Dr. Pemmaraju and the head of the transplant department at MD Anderson, Dr. Muzaffar Qazalbash, put me on a four-day dosage of toxic chemo. Would it work? Would a second transplant save my life?

Once I had completed my work for NBC Sports at the 2001 Wimbledon Championships in England, I announced to Stacy, who had come with me, that I was going to fulfill a bucket-list item by running with the bulls in Pamplona, Spain. She knew me well enough to know there was little to convince me to not do something on which my heart was set, so we flew to Barcelona and rented a car for what we thought would be a two-hour drive. I don't like long car rides. Never have. For someone like me who is always on the go and who is always ready for the next thing, sitting in a car for more than an hour or two is like being held hostage by time, so when we passed hour number two and were still on the road, I turned the car around and drove back to Barcelona, and we *flew* to Pamplona.

For those of you who have been to New Orleans for Mardi Gras or Brazil for Carnival, the festival surrounding the Running of the Bulls is ten times as crazy, festive, and full of life. The city itself was overrun by tourists, tens of thousands of people dressed in white from head to toe. We were the victims of an attempted pickpocketing shortly after arriving, which I guess should not have surprised us. After checking into a hotel in the center of town, I began to plan my attack the following day. I would dress in all white and make my way to the starting gates very early; Stacy would meet me at the bottom of the course near the finish.

I was up at the crack of dawn and even managed to get in a little run before the town fully came alive. I was in Pamplona for the first time, and I am sure that we rookies stood out, if not for our confused looks, then for our rushing to the starting line. See, I figured I could give myself a safe cushion if I started to run downhill before they opened the gates and let the bulls loose. What I didn't know is that anyone who tries to take off running before the bulls are released gets dragged back and thrown in the front again.

My heart was pounding as the gates holding in the animals swung open and a loud roar consumed the street. I ran. Ran like Forrest Gump and didn't stop running. I kept running past the throngs along the street, past the bakeries and shops that lined the course. I ran until I saw Stacy at what I thought was the finish line. When I stopped for her to take a picture, I glanced behind me and saw no running bulls. I didn't even see bulls. I had outrun them all. Of course, as per custom, I was not allowed to exit the street until the bulls had passed me by, so I waited . . . and waited. Suddenly, like a large wave building as it nears the shoreline, a flood of screaming men dressed in white, some covered in blood, came flowing into my path, with the raging animals mixed in among them.

The wave carried us all into the town's stadium, where organizers unleashed another group of bulls onto the crowd. I found a barrel on the turf and jumped inside.

Never again, I thought to myself.

But sitting at MD Anderson, I found myself thinking that if I outran the bulls, I could outrun leukemia. And yet again, I would have my son running alongside me.

20

A Second Chance

My dad's relapse with leukemia in the spring of 2015 brought about a sense of guilt and failure that I hadn't seen coming. The image of my dad and me celebrating in the parking lot after the first transplant replayed over and over again in my head. The more it replayed itself, the more I missed that feeling. I had hope, but I was playing an exhausting game of tag with my confidence.

My uncle—my dad's sister's husband—had fallen ill while visiting my father and ultimately died of congenital heart failure on May 9 at Northside. At his funeral, I was consumed by a deep-rooted helplessness, and I felt the pain of my entire family at once. The first transplant meant more to me than just being a donor for my dad—I had felt like I was saving my family in a sense, and now I was watching it fall apart again.

I tried to mimic my father's positive approach in any radio or television interview I was asked to do about my father's battle, but the void between the words coming out of my mouth and my actual feelings kept expanding.

I was hopeful when Dad and Stacy went to MD Anderson, because I knew it was the best hospital in the world.

I was at the Atlanta Falcons' headquarters on May 26 to wrap up my final day of covering their spring practice. I went home that night to start packing for a trip to visit my sister in Tampa the next morning. As I was packing, my cell phone rang.

"Junior," said Stacy, "your father needs you."

Stacy explained to me the direness of the situation for Dad and the immediate need to do a second bone marrow transplant. Though the first attempt using my marrow had failed, doctors wanted to try a second time but with a different procedure. Before our conversation ended, there was an 8:00 a.m. flight to Houston already booked and an itinerary waiting in my inbox from MD Anderson, laying out the first three days of the donation process, as this time around things would be much different.

I arrived in Houston less than twelve hours later. Dad's condition was deteriorating, and the odds were stacked against us more than at any time before, but knowing I had another chance made me feel alive again.

I had forty minutes before my first appointment, not even enough time to check in at my hotel and drop off my luggage. I rushed through the terminal until I was stopped in my tracks by a massive wall-to-wall MD Anderson advertisement overhead: ONE GOAL: CANCER. I let that simple message resonate as I took a deep breath. I felt a surge of focus and began the long walk.

I was fascinated by the hospital's efficiency and

organization. With my donor checklist in hand, I migrated
with hundreds of other patients from floor to floor and
building to building. There was a process at MD Anderson,
not the waiting lines I was accustomed to. To get my
blood work done, I'd scan my wristband at the front desk
and get handed an index-card-size form with printed
labels ready to be peeled off and slapped on whatever
number of vials my card called for that day. I was funneled
into a room with several nurses who were perched at their
stations and ready to go. Eye contact and an empty chair
were the inherent language. Like a pit crew, they had us in
and out before I could even suggest how relieved I was to
be done with my blood work—at least for the first day.

Instead of harvesting the transplant directly from my
bone marrow, like the first time around, this transplant
process consisted of daily shots that would generate
enough white blood cells to escape into my bloodstream.
This allowed them to avoid having to drill through my
bone to reach the stem cells.

The daily labs were done in the mornings, followed by
meetings with the doctors who would be performing the
stem cell harvest. I received Neupogen shots in my abdomen each day, which were used to boost my stem cell and
white blood cell counts. I Googled Neupogen and learned
that a donor can administer the shots himself; the doctors
actually asked if I wanted to jam a needle into my own
stomach each time. Most of the time, I just laughed
uncomfortably at the question. Each day, I could feel my
legs getting fuller with blood, my body feeling heavier,
and my chest feeling tighter. The discomfort meant that it
was working.

I spent the time between my appointments in my dad's

hospital room until he couldn't take it anymore and demanded that I "go have fun instead." I played golf in Houston, toured the city's sports venues, strolled Rice University's campus, and even squeezed in an Astros game and a trip to the Museum of Natural Science. During my visit to the museum, a Texas flash flood came out of nowhere and left me locked in the exhibits for hours after closing. My dad watched the weather reports from his room and laughed with me over the phone as I staved off my hunger with the only source of food I could find—rock candy from the museum gift shop.

Every day, Dad would go for a walk at around the same time, and I made it a point to be there during his only time out of his room. The walks were therapeutic for both of us. With his gown and mask much more loosely fitted than any doctor would advise, he led the way. He wheeled a tower of tubes, cords, chemo, and monitors through the longest and most scenic path he could devise. There was no way that this was what the doctors had in mind when they told him he could go for a walk, but it was exactly what I expected. We hit every corner of the hospital, including a secret workout room where he rode the bike each day. We always ended the walks outside in the hospital garden, where Dad had found a bench he liked. Once we were situated, he worked, made phone calls, and enjoyed the groomed landscape surrounding the hospital until the doctors urged him to return or he had his next treatment or check-in. The humidity and scorching heat were smothering, but since he didn't mind, I didn't either.

Every previous trip I'd gone on with my dad had been either a party or work; that was all we knew. Golf trips, barhopping, trips to the Bahamas, playoff basketball—that was the only pace of life we'd known before this. Now the two of us were sharing a moment of our lives where the future was too unpredictable and overwhelming to even exist and there was nothing else in the world to be doing. The only thing we did know was that speaking about leukemia or the hospital or anything to do with the indoors would have interrupted the moment. During our walks, our conversations bounced around from mapping out his favorite places in Houston to admiring the pigeons that were stalking us for food.

The pigeons reminded us of the Olympics in 1996, when the City of Atlanta brutally purged the pigeon population. We also reminisced about a round of golf in Malibu where Dad's fuchsia flower-printed shorts had drawn aerial attacks from hungry hummingbirds the entire round. When we finished our conversation or when it was time to leave, we would make the walk back up to his room. I'd change back into a gown and mask and Dad would return to a rotating wardrobe of warm-ups and team T-shirts, ready to check off another day.

With enough Neupogen in my body to saturate my bloodstream plus another two shots for assurance, doctors moved me on to the harvesting process, or apheresis, on the morning of June 2. "Apheresis" is a word that still triggers a Pavlovian urge to roll down my sleeves and cringe, but in the medical world, it is a technology that separates the blood of the donor to collect a particular substance (stem cells in our case) and returns the remaining blood to the donor.

The first thing I noticed during the apheresis procedure was that the needles looked more like ballpoint pens. Nurses forced them deep into each arm as I clenched my teeth and realized how much more painful this would be than the first transplant. I watched my entire bloodstream filter through the noisy dialysis machine next to me for hours as the blood ran out one arm, filtered through the machine's network of tubes, and then reentered my body through my other arm. If the blood started to drizzle out of my arm more slowly than was required, the machine would sound an alarm and I would have to squeeze more quickly the stress balls that I was rhythmically pumping the entire time. I thought I had overcome my fear of needles, but I was pushing streams of blood out of my own body and I couldn't ignore it. I tried to stay as still as possible, but my body became more uncomfortably tense the longer I tried not to move.

When it was over for the day, the nurses pulled the needles out and sent the collected cells to the lab to see if they had extracted enough of them for the transplant. Confident in my relative youth as a donor, my own immune system, and my swollen stomach from a week of shots, I believed the process was done.

When I returned the next morning, however, I was greeted with two more Neupogen shots and a new room number—they were not even halfway to the threshold they were aiming to collect. At least by now the nurses knew better than to ask me if I wanted to give myself the shots that day. My bruised veins ached as I lay down and the nurses repeated the same process. More needles, more blood, more squeezing balls. I was haunted by the thought of having to schedule another flight and go through this yet another time if they didn't get enough.

On June 4, I got the news I was waiting for. Doctors had collected the targeted six million stem cells and then

154 • LIVING OUT LOUD

some. With a flight to catch later that day, I rushed up to Dad's room to relay the good news and to say goodbye. Before I could enjoy my relief, however, a team of doctors entered the room behind me and blindsided us all with the most unexpected and difficult news I had heard since Dad's original diagnosis.

The chemotherapy drugs that he had been on since arriving at MD Anderson a few weeks earlier weren't working, and his leukemia blasts had skyrocketed to a lethal 74 percent. Doctors won't even consider a transplant unless the blasts are below 8 percent, so the transplant was on hold. The issue now was whether doctors could save my dad's life. As Dad and the doctors discussed options, I sat quietly off to the side, stunned. I wanted to stay, but Dad insisted that I had done enough and should go catch my flight.

Seeing that he wanted—maybe even needed—me to leave, I respected his wishes, but I left the hospital armed only with the knowledge that my efforts and stem cell donation would be useless without some sort of miracle. My dad was dying.

21

RELENTLESS

When Dr. Pemmaraju told me that my blasts were up to 74 percent, it was a left hook; despite my fight gene, I knew the harsh reality of the situation. My leukemia was aggressive and was finding new ways to fight me. I had spontaneous bleeding from my mouth and nose, and I was dangerously low on platelets. The chemo had weakened my immune system, and I had little strength left to fight.

"If untreated, this relapse of AML, after a transplant, can take your life in just weeks to a month," Dr. Pemmaraju told me, "unless we find a way to extend your life."

Weeks to a month. Yeah, right, just like Dr. Holland had given me three weeks in March. What's with doctors putting a stopwatch on *my* life?

"But I have a plan," said Dr. P, and my eyes lit up. "We will get you into a new, aggressive clinical trial, and we will get this fixed *together*."

I believed him—that not only did he know what he was

doing but that he was doing it *with* us, not just *for* us. He went to work and identified the right trial for me to start right away, and the nurse began the hefty paperwork.

"This is your best chance for remission," he reminded me as I griped through the bureaucratic process.

Six hours later, Dr. Pemmaraju returned with devastating news. The trial he wanted me in, with a drug that was my last hope for survival, did not accept AML patients who had already had a stem cell transplant.

"No way!" Stacy jumped in. "They are taking away Craig's only chance. I suggest we figure this out. I know that with a little more paperwork and phone calls we can get this done . . . and we have thirty minutes to make it happen and we won't take no for an answer."

There was a second of silence as Dr. Pemmaraju's eyes darted quickly from Stacy to me.

"Great, let's go for it!" he said. "Let's do it!"

With that, Dr. Pemmaraju disappeared and we waited. Stacy and I held hands, and she kept telling me that we would get into the trial and it would work and I would be fine. Her confidence and reassurances meant the world to me. Dr. P returned to the room a few minutes later with an update. The biotech company whose drug was used in the clinical trial was based in Japan, and it would not make an exception to include me in the trial unless its full board gave their blessing. Dr. Qazilbash, said no to Dr. Pemmaraju's wanting to try to get a board vote. He told him I couldn't be part of the trial.

"I don't care," said Stacy. "Make it happen."

So, again, Dr. Pemmaraju went to work. A few hours later, he told us the board would consider my case but that they would not meet until Monday, as we were entering the weekend.

Will I make it till Monday? I asked myself. But then I thought, *Of course I will.*

"Relentless" is a kind adjective that some folks use in describing me. I guess it's much more of a compliment than "pest" or "pain in the ass," which I have also heard throughout my career. My dogged pursuit of the story—of information—dates way back to my first job as a radio update anchor in Sarasota, where I would call the city's mayor at 5:00 a.m. to confirm something I had heard the night before.

When two-sport star Deion Sanders was traded from the Cincinnati Reds to the San Francisco Giants in August 1995, I wanted to be the first to hear from "Prime Time," who declined to speak to the media. A few decades earlier, I had broadcast ten-year-old Deion's Pee Wee football games in Fort Myers, getting $25 a game from sponsor Pepsi to do so. And yes, Deion was amazing even as a ten-year-old. I used that connection to track down his mother, Ms. Connie Knight, living in Florida, to help me secure an interview with Deion.

In March 1997, Shaquille O'Neal was a member of the Los Angeles Lakers, having signed as a free agent the previous summer, ending his time with the Orlando Magic. The Lakers were on the road to face Shaq's old team, but an injured Shaq wasn't talking to the media, choosing instead to seclude himself at his Isleworth mansion, outside Orlando. I knew the security guards at the gate would never let me and my television crew in, so I had to get creative.

We drove around the lake until we found a boat launch spot, where I noticed a man struggling to get his motorboat into the water. I offered assistance, with a catch—he had to pilot me to

Shaq's house. So with assistance from the crew, we launched the boat and drove around the waters of Isleworth until we spotted Shaq's boat, docked out back of his house. Shaq was outside shooting hoops, but despite my most convincing pleas, he still refused to talk. I pleaded with the big guy that my crew and I had gone through so much effort just to get there—could he *please* talk with me?

"Next time I am going to send my alligators on you," he told me.

But I got the interview.

I guess if any athlete really thought I was a pain in the ass, it was Mr. October, the great New York Yankee Reggie Jackson. As a cub reporter in Fort Myers, I would cover the Yankees when they came to town, and Reggie was always unavailable. He would drive up to the ball field right before the start of the game in a Rolls-Royce and brush right past the young, adoring fans asking for autographs. As a reporter, I wanted the interview, so I followed the Yankees from Fort Myers to Sarasota to Fort Lauderdale, always trying to talk to him on his way in or out.

At this point in my career, I was still a one-man band, lugging around a big old wooden tripod and a rudimentary video camera that weighed a ton. Everywhere I went, so, too, went my equipment. During a Yankees game in Fort Myers, I decided that today would be it. I knew that Reggie had a habit of changing clothes and leaving the park early, well before his teammates. So I set up my tripod and camera a few feet behind his Rolls-Royce, clearly blocking his exit.

"Reggie, I am all set up," I pleaded with a smile.

He shrugged, scowled, and insisted he didn't have time.

"Please. Just a few questions?"

And in the parking lot in Fort Myers I got my interview.

Sometimes you need to create your own luck. Ever since then, whenever Reggie has spotted me at a game or a press conference, he's smiled and said, "One-man gang."

Relentless.

As it turns out, Stacy was relentless, too. And that drive had at least given us hope for the weekend.

22

DANIEL AND BRANDON

The wait over the weekend was excruciating. I was dying, and my only hope rested with a group of Japanese businessmen whom I had never met, in a land far, far away. They didn't know me, didn't know how much my bride and kids needed me, and surely didn't know or care that I was a sports broadcaster. The odds were against us, but haven't they been for a long time?

Late Monday, a miracle happened when we received the news: we were a go.

Dr. Pemmaraju, Stacy, the nurses, and everyone else on our team was thrilled, but Dr. P laid out all the risks.

"We will do fourteen straight days of chemotherapy, twenty-four hours a day," he said. "There is a risk that the chemo may shut down your organs and kill you—but you *will have a chance.*"

Never before, anywhere in the world, Dr. Pemmaraju explained, had this intensity of chemo been tried on an AML patient in my condition. Either the chemo would kill me or the leukemia would, or maybe, just maybe, I could be a miracle.

So on June 9, I started fourteen days of around-the-clock

chemo. Because I had declined to be on the isolation floor and was staying on the "leukemia floor," I had a bit more freedom. So much freedom, in fact, that while doctors and nurses told me I couldn't leave the hospital, Stacy and I would grab a few minutes every day and walk around outside in the courtyard, gowned, gloved, and masked, with my ongoing chemo rig in tow. Just feeling the fresh air and watching the clouds move against a crystal blue sky was all I needed. As for the chemo, I felt remarkably well and my body was holding up, except for the loss of hair.

On June 23, fourteen days later, the doctors stopped the chemo. I was still alive, which was great news, but we wouldn't know if the chemo had worked until a biopsy. (As I write this book, the number of aspirations and biopsies has reached twenty-three and counting, and I have become quite an authority on this barbaric procedure.)

Two days later, I had a bone marrow biopsy, and I actually looked forward to it, because I knew it was the only way to know if my blasts had gone down. The results came back: my blasts were down to zero percent. That's right. In two weeks, I went from near-death 74 percent blasts to absolutely zero. The miraculous chemo trial had worked. Stacy's pushing, Dr. Pemmaraju's advocacy, and a Japanese drug had saved my life.

Now that I was back in remission, the doctors worked toward a second stem cell transplant around July 4, ten days away, having already harvested the necessary stem cells from Junior. Since I was in remission, Dr. Pemmaraju allowed me to continue my treatment on an outpatient basis, so at least Stacy and I found some normalcy at the Marriott Medical Center. But on July 3, the night before the scheduled transplant procedure, I woke up in the middle of the night at the hotel with a fever, chills, and vomiting. Stacy got me right to the emergency room, and within hours, doctors had confirmed that I had come down with an infection—pseudomonas, a deadly type of bacterial infection for immune-compromised patients like me— and this would postpone the transplant. I was devastated. I had persevered through the ups and downs, through the fourteen days of chemo, and I was looking forward to another rebirth with a second transplant. I pouted for about one minute and then became re-determined to rid my body of the infection. *You're supposed to be dead, remember?* The power of positive thinking (and medicine) worked, the infection soon went away, and the transplant was back on.

I began five days of chemo, followed by a few days off, then two last days of chemo. On July 19, fifteen days after the initial scheduled transplant, I received my son's bone marrow—again— and started the clock ticking on the next hundred days. MD Anderson did not allow patients to leave the hospital in the hundred days after a transplant, as Northside had allowed, so I wasn't going anywhere. In my head, I figured if I did well enough after thirty days, I would be released on good behavior, against hospital protocol.

Every day in July, Stacy was at my side, holding my hand, peppering the nurses with questions or laughing at my silly jokes, and every night she would sleep on an air mattress in my room. I spent my days watching television, mostly sports—tennis, golf, baseball, you name it. But I also became a loyal watcher of *The Andy Griffith Show*, *Gunsmoke*, and *Bonanza* reruns. I had watched those shows in the 1960s and also when Turner aired *The Andy Griffith Show* during Atlanta Braves' rain delays. (When the game resumed and Turner switched back to baseball, legendary announcer Skip Caray would let the audience know what happened in the remaining minutes of the episode.) Now I could tell you about every episode, every character, and what the writers should have done differently.

During my daily walks around the seventeenth floor in my weakened state, I would pass the exercise room, and I always smirked and chuckled when I saw patients in their gowns or robes, sitting in chairs and doing arm exercises like it was Thursday morning at a South Florida retirement home. Canes and walkers sat nearby.

"You should join the class," said Dr. Pemmaraju one morning as he saw me watching them.

He said it would help build back my strength and agility.

Uh, no thanks, Doc, I thought to myself, but then I caught myself in the window separating me from the room. Maybe he had a point.

The class was surprisingly fun, proved to be great for my balance, and got the circulation going. And not only did I love our instructor, a physical therapist named Kim Presson, but I got to know a few of my classmates. Right off the bat, I became particularly close with Daniel and Brandon. Daniel was a gentleman from Brazil in his late forties who, when he wasn't living at MDA, resided in Miami. He had already been through one transplant and was looking forward to getting out to go back and live with his daughter in Miami. As for Brandon, he was a fun, lively guy in his thirties, and we instantly connected over a mutual love of sports. He had already had a transplant and was in remission, awaiting the doctor's permission to go home. His new bride awaited him, as they had moved up their wedding date to before his transplant.

"When I get home," he would say, "I'm going on my honeymoon!"

Seeing these two guys was a key component in getting me to

class. As we went through our exercises, we'd chat about sports or about getting out of the hospital. We shared laughs about the humbling experience of our exercise regimen—no one watching would mistake us for Mr. Olympias in training—but the seriousness of our situation made deeper connection inevitable.

As Daniel's leukemia worsened, he had no choice but to sell the Miami house to help pay his medical bills, just as he had sold his house in Brazil to come to MD Anderson. We talked about the limits of insurance coverage and the nonmedical costs, like hotels, flights, and food, which piled up quickly. He also confided in me that the physical and emotional struggle of his battle was taking a toll, and he was worried about the financial burden he'd be leaving behind for his family in case he didn't make it.

I'd hear none of it. I channeled Willie the Wildcat and hammed it up, getting him to laugh and hoping beyond all hope I might make him a believer in himself again.

One day, Daniel came to my room, something he rarely did, with a dour look on his face.

"I'm done," he shared with me.

"What do you mean you are done?"

"They been telling me for weeks that I was getting out. Now they want to do another treatment and keep me here. More tests. I am not going to do it," he said in his broken English.

"Where are you going to go?" I asked.

"I don't know. I just want out of here. I don't have any place to go. I will live under a bridge in Houston."

I could see the determination in his eyes and hear the conviction in his voice.

"But, Daniel, stay a little longer. They know what they are doing. They can help you here. Don't walk out now."

"I'm done. This never ends. I am not doing it anymore."

"Don't you think the doctors know what they are doing?"

I couldn't believe what I was hearing. Daniel had fought the battle for so long; why give up now? It was like being at mile 25 in a marathon and deciding to stop running. But the nurses, doctors, and I could not convince him to stay. He packed his belongings and walked right out of the hospital. I never saw him again.

The power of positive thinking is a crucial element of my survival. I have witnessed firsthand the healing power of optimism. Over the course of my many lengthy stays at Northside Hospital and MD Anderson, I have seen fellow patients, many of whom I'd grown quite close to, give up, stop fighting, and succumb within a matter of days. I will never pass judgment on others' decisions, but the moment they stopped believing in tomorrow, the end came. For some, the emotions were too much, or it was the financial burden left on their families, or simply that the will to live had slowly been beaten down by an incurable disease.

It reaffirmed my determination to raise awareness for leukemia and to help raise funds to find a cure. Patients like Daniel should not be faced with life-and-death decisions because of the *costs* of those decisions. I would fight for others who couldn't.

As for Brandon and me, we plowed through, losing ourselves in our exercise routine and regular small talk. "When I get outta here . . ." was his mantra, and his humor, positivity, and courage reinforced my own.

One day in class, Brandon began bleeding profusely from his nose. An infection had taken hold. The event itself—with orderlies and nurses rushing him out of the exercise room—was scary, but soon we were visiting each other's rooms, continuing our banter, reviewing the day in sports like a couple of coanchors. "When I get outta here . . ."

As the weeks went by, our interactions became less frequent. Brandon wasn't in exercise class, and I got caught up in my own day-to-day of trying to stay alive. After exercise class one day, I went to visit him in his room. I really wanted to see him, if only selfishly, to pep me up.

The room was empty.

"Excuse me," I asked a nurse, "where is Brandon in room 1744?"

Her look said it all.

Though MD Anderson does not allow transplant patients to leave in the first hundred days, doctors can make exceptions for patients who have recovered and are strong enough to move to outpatient treatment after thirty days, and that was just what Dr. Pemmaraju allowed me to do. Stacy was with me until early August, when the kids returned to school and she began a weekly Houston-to-Atlanta commute. Dr. Pemmaraju even let us go to our second home in Orlando for a few days and allowed me to return to Atlanta so I could see the kids.

A hematoma—an abnormal collection of blood outside of a blood vessel—developed in my brain, but after careful analysis, doctors did not think it was dangerous. In late August, I was still in remission, and Dr. Pemmaraju started me on a steady but low dosage of Vidaza as a precaution. There were five-day cycles of Vidaza, which included two shots a day. The Vidaza was not simply flushed into my body via an IV—it could be more effective if inserted directly into my abdomen. So each of the five days, a nurse would come in with a cool pack of the medicine, which had to be warmed immediately before it was inserted into two needles, which were then thrust into my abdomen. The nurses alternated the shot locations each day—one day two shots on the left, the next day two shots on the right.

In addition to the precautionary chemo, the transplant was working, and I looked ahead to the start of the NBA season in October, although, armed with the knowledge of what had happened in 2014, I was prepared for anything.

23

SLEW

I have been an automobile aficionado since I received my Illinois driver's license in 1967. I was fascinated and captivated by the sleek styles, the bright colors, the speed of cars. Over the years I have owned a 1935 Rolls-Royce Bentley, a 1959 Mercedes-Benz 190SL, a 1963 Ford Galaxie convertible, a 1964 MGB, a 1966 Jaguar XKE, a 1968 Pontiac GTO, a 1973 Mercury Cougar convertible, a 1984 Cadillac Eldorado convertible, a 1986 Chevy Malibu convertible, and a 1990 Corvette convertible, which I still drive to this day.

I collect *everything*. There are my baseball cards from childhood, which sit, pristine, in my house; my nickel collection, which I recently passed on to Ryan; *every* press pass I've ever been issued; and the Kissing Bandit's bra, supported by two large Pop-a-Shot basketballs. As they say, it's a long story, but the short of it is that Morganna, the Kissing Bandit, who earned her nickname for running onto various fields and courts during games to kiss sports stars, and I became friends way back in the mid-1970s, when she would attend spring training—

she was a baseball fanatic. A few times over the years, I have had to get her out of various jails for her antics, and she gave me a bra as a gesture of thanks.

Near the Morganna bra in the case in the basement, in a small glass container, also sits one of my more unique items— thirty-nine-year-old horse poop.

I fell in love with horse racing as a young man working in Fort Myers. As it happened, a veterinarian named Jim Hill and his wife, Sally, had lived in the area before and were well-known in horse racing circles, not only for Jim's work in the field but also as the co-owners of thirteen horses, in partnership with their friends Karen and Mickey Taylor, from Seattle. Jim was a kind man with a competitive streak, and he would teach me the finer points of the sport—from jockey weights to the thickness of the turf, from the importance of bloodlines to the importance of betting lines.

One of the horses the Hills and Taylors owned was a dark-brown youngster with great potential whom they named Seattle Slew, after the name of the Washington city and the sloughs of South Florida. The colt won his first three races of 1977 and was the favorite heading into the storied Kentucky Derby at Churchill Downs in Louisville. My employer, WINK-TV, had no interest in spending money to send me to Louisville to cover a horse race, so instead I tracked down Jim Hill's mother, who still lived in Fort Myers, and watched the race with her, capturing her reaction on tape. I did the same during Slew's Preakness victory in Baltimore a few weeks later. But there was no way I was going to miss his shot at the Triple Crown at Belmont Park in New York.

I flew to New York on Friday morning, the day before the

race, and quickly caught up with Dr. Hill, trainer Billy Turner, and the Slew crew. I snuck away a few times in the afternoon to place bets at the windows on the Friday races, aided by inside tips from Slew's jockey, Jean Cruguet. At night, as the park and the field emptied, Billy, the crew, and I walked across from the stables to Esposito's Tavern for some late-night drinks and tall tales. After shots of vodka and a few too many beers, Billy suggested that instead of spending money on a hotel room, I should sleep in the stables with Slew, as stable crews would be watching him all night. I left Esposito's after midnight and walked to Barn 54, where Cecil Murphy was on duty.

"There," Cecil said, pointing with his outstretched arm to a small wooden bench a few feet from the horse, indicating that this was my bed for the night. I grabbed a horse blanket for covers and used a pinch of hay for a pillow. And there I slept for a few hours, next to one of the greatest racehorses that ever lived.

I woke at 4:00 a.m. with the trainers to feed Slew breakfast and to take him for a walk. Before we left the stable, I noticed a pile of Slew's excrement resting comfortably on the hay. Knowing just how incredible the moment was, I grabbed one of Dr. Hill's plastic surgical gloves and put some Slew poop in it to take back to Florida with me. Along with the $1,760 I won on an $800 bet when Slew finished first at the Belmont.

The Seattle Slew story has made its rounds over the years and, along with my Hank Aaron story, constitutes the majority of interest in my work, which at first blush is surprising, given that I'm most visible on the NBA sidelines. But on further thought, it's not all that surprising. They're really classic examples of not just bearing witness to history but participating in it, and I guess, on reflection, my drive to be part of the sports culture about which I've always been so passionate has compelled me to create my own luck.

I really try to impress this idea on my kids. Life is wonderful and fun and full of adventure, and with a little ingenuity, you can put yourself in the right place and good things will happen.

"But there are boundaries," I can hear the Dilberts say. "Rules."

Rules are for people without brains. Simply use common sense, and when you need to find a way, find a way. Whether it's breaking into a water slide at night in the Bahamas (which I do often with my youngest kids) or bringing home a rattlesnake to share with the oldest kids when they were young, I have always found ways to have fun. (And lived to tell the tale—that's important, too.)

MAYBE THIS TIME I AM BACK

In October 2015, past the one-hundred-day post-transplant mark and with my leukemia still in remission, Dr. Pemmaraju cleared me to return to work. The second transplant seemed to be working: all of the blood indicators were in my favor, and there were no signs of leukemia blasts. It had been a long eighteen-month battle, but this time I was sure that I had defeated the enemy.

My first game back was New Orleans at Golden State on opening night, on which the Warriors received their championship rings for winning the title in June. It was a big night for them—and for me. I had been looking forward to it since my transplant in July and had spent extra time picking out *just* the right outfit. I decided on an orange ensemble, to signify the fight against leukemia. I stuck to my usual game routine in San Francisco, which meant day-before interviews with coaches and players, a crab salad sandwich, and a walk (instead of a run) along the water. It felt so good to be back on the road and back on the air working, and the words of encouragement I received from the NBA family were uplifting.

> Craig . . . congrats on finishing your treatments early! Been thinking about you and praying for you and your family. Can't wait to see you back on the sidelines soon!!!
> —Erik Spoelstra, head coach, Miami Heat

My schedule was full of upcoming games, and I did nothing to slow it down. According to blood tests in mid-November, my blasts levels had risen from 0 to 2 percent, which was still considered to be in remission. Not great news, but nothing to be too concerned about. Dr. Pemmaraju put me on a mild dosage of chemo a few days a month. I continued to travel and work, and the outpouring of encouragement from gracious friends and strangers alike often moved me to the edge of tears. Men and women of all ages and colors would share their own families' battles with cancer or simply offer up prayers for me. I started to understand the impact my fight was having on others.

In December, with more than a dozen NBA games under my belt, I underwent yet another bone marrow biopsy at MD Anderson, and the blasts had risen to 3 percent. At that point, Stacy, Dr. Pemmaraju, and I had the "talk" about next steps; with the blasts increasing for another month in a row, the leukemia could be on its way back. We discussed a potential third stem cell transplant, though Dr. Pemmaraju said it would be quite rare. He decided he wanted to give the chemo one more month and then reassess in January.

At this point in my long battle, Stacy and I met good news

and bad news with the same reaction: hope for the best, but whatever comes our way, we will fight it.

On several occasions I had been given weeks to live, yet here I was, back on the road and enjoying life. Was I a medical miracle? I will leave that to others to decide. Did my determined and positive approach help? I'll never stop believing it did.

I was keeping busy traveling from city to city for games. From Los Angeles to San Antonio, Cleveland to Miami, the miles piled up.

The January biopsy revealed that the blast count had increased from 3 percent to 22 percent, an alarming jump in just four weeks. We knew that we needed to try a different approach to hold off the aggressive disease, and Dr. Pemmaraju researched ongoing clinical trials that might work. It had been eight months after my first transplant that I had relapsed, and seven months after the second one. There is a much greater survival rate if a patient can remain in remission for a minimum of twelve months after a transplant, and I was headed in the wrong direction.

During my testing and visit in early February, the biopsy revealed that the blasts had gone up from 22 percent to 28 percent. Dr. Pemmaraju had a new plan. After I returned from the NBA All-Star Game in Toronto in mid-February, I would start eight straight days of a combination of chemotherapy and immunotherapy. I would continue with the Vidaza for my chemo, but we would add in Lirilumab, a proven cancer immunotherapy killer but one that had never before been tried on a leukemia patient in my stage, and a drug not yet approved by the FDA to treat leukemia.

"Let's do it," I told Dr. Pemmaraju without hesitation. Honestly, we had few choices.

(Fortunately, when we started the Vidaza-Lirilumab cycle,

the doctors decided to increase the strength of the Vidaza, and therefore I could receive it via IV instead of abdomen shots.)

As Stacy, the kids, and I headed to Toronto for All-Star Weekend, I was no longer in remission, and Stacy and I decided not to share the relapse news with anybody. That meant spending the weekend with my family and seeing old NBA friends but not being able to share what was really going on. I have always been an honest person—sometimes to my immediate detriment (oh, the interviews I *could've* gotten if I'd just kept my mouth closed!)—and I worried about not being completely truthful with friends and strangers in Toronto when they would inevitably ask me how I was doing. I understood by now that people were rooting for me and that there were people very tied to the battle I was waging, but I decided that my responsibility was to just keep fighting for my life.

"How you feeling?" I was asked dozens of times by players, coaches, and strangers that weekend.

"Doing the best I can," I'd respond.

I did everything possible to avoid being untruthful. There were times that weekend when it was uncomfortable, but I tried to not think about it, distracted by family and the All-Star festivities. It was Kobe Bryant's farewell All-Star Game and the passing of the torch to Steph Curry, and I loved every minute of it.

We had a long-scheduled family vacation to our home in Orlando immediately after Toronto, as the kids were off from school, but I had to return to Houston on Monday morning. Despite her resistance, Stacy agreed to go ahead to Orlando so she and the kids could enjoy a short respite.

The new combination of Vidaza and Lirilumab would not show much of an impact for weeks, so we knew we were unlikely to see a marked improvement anytime soon. I also knew that the drugs were unlikely to get me back into remission. At best, it would slow down the aggressiveness of the leukemia or maybe even lessen it a bit, but we knew that this was only a bandage. The day after the All-Star Game, I was full steam ahead starting my first day of yet another game plan. I was not scheduled to do any games that week anyway, as I had taken off time for the family vacation.

In late February, my best and oldest friend from Batavia, John Clark, came down to visit me in Houston, and we got in a round of eighteen.

"Hondo," I blurted out, using the nickname I liked to call him, "we should do this again. And you know what? I am going to do everything in my power to make it to Jenny's wedding." His daughter was scheduled to be married in Batavia in July.

Being on the golf course took my mind away from the aggressive return of the leukemia, but it hit me like a brick later that day as Hondo and I rode down in an elevator at MD Anderson.

"This is just no way to live," I admitted, knowing what lay ahead in the coming months. For a brief moment, I questioned whether I really could do it. But as had happened often in my life, the negative thought was fleeting, and soon my resolve and determination returned.

Finally, Dr. Pemmaraju gave me the go-ahead to go back to work on February 25 for an Oklahoma City game in New Orleans. I was back on the road, living my life, but every few days I needed a blood transfusion and new platelets just to stay alive. I was swimming upstream.

On March 10, producers from HBO's *Real Sports with Bryant Gumbel* reached out to see if I would be interested in being the subject of a feature profile. Before agreeing to sit for an interview with reporter Bernard Goldberg, I wanted to make sure that the story would focus on the positives and not the negatives, as I wanted AML awareness to be the focus, not to see a pity story. Two days later, HBO and Bernie were in my home in Canton, Georgia, interviewing me and Junior for the story. I shared publicly for the first time that my leukemia was no longer in remission, and I was candid about my prognosis.

> I [said to the doctors], "I know, what are the chances?" And [the doctors said], "Well, you've got normally three to six months to live. But somebody may only have a week. Somebody may have five years. You could be the first one to five years."
>
> I go, "Well, whatever it takes." I'm not going to be that three to six months. I'm going to be that five years. I'm going to make medical history. . . . I'm fighting this thing to the end. I have too much to do.

I returned to Houston for my second eight-day cycle, and the blasts were up to 36 percent. The treatment appeared to not be working, and doctors were keeping an eye on my kidneys, spleen, and heart, as the two chemo drugs were highly toxic.

When the HBO story aired on March 22, the headline, of course, was that I had only months to live. What was not made clear in the HBO piece was that the three-to-six-month time frame was for someone with aggressive leukemia who was not receiving any treatment. I had to clarify the prognosis in a statement the following day.

I had no idea of the impact that the *Real Sports* story would have on my own story. Suddenly players, coaches, long-lost friends from Batavia, strangers, golfing buddies—everyone knew, and everyone thought I was near the end. I received letters that, though kind in intent, were ominous.

You have had a great life. There is a better life afterwards.
You were a great broadcaster and you will be sorely missed.

I know they meant well, and I wasn't upset, but it was almost like reading your own obituary.

The only question or comment that really upset me was from John, my best friend for more than sixty years. With good intentions, he asked me if I had my "things in order."

"Are you giving up on me?" I shot back.

He clarified his meaning. "Estate, will, finances . . ."

I thought pretty deeply about why this, of all the inauspicious commentary, bothered me.

Ego. I *always* have my things in order.

It makes me laugh to write that, but there's some takeaway there. Have your "things in order" so that, when you have to, you can focus on the actual fight.

In the days and weeks after the HBO story aired, I got noticed on the street and stopped by people more frequently—I saw heads turn, even if I pretended not to notice. But when I walked into an NBA arena for my assignments—I kept up a pretty full work schedule—the magnitude and reach of the story couldn't be ignored.

In early April, before the start of the NBA playoffs, I was heading back to MD Anderson for eight days. Just before my return to Houston, Stacy and I took the kids to the Turks and Caicos for a long weekend—a place we had always wanted to go but had kept putting off. We had a great time, snorkeling, picking up seashells, and playing in the ocean, but I also caught myself out of breath and weak. By the time I got to MDA, I knew that I needed transfusions and platelets. And I was right: my blasts were up to 36 percent. Things were getting worse, not better, and I didn't know how long my body would put up the fight.

25

Searching for Answers

The first year of my father's leukemia was a brand-new growing process for me that I came to embrace. By the time we made it through the second transplant, however, I could feel myself slowly unraveling.

When my father miraculously made his way back to the sideline again in October, it was an intoxicating blend of emotions for me. Sports became bearable again. I could enjoy watching them after a long day of work again, knowing Dad was back. My own hope had been restored. Each time he went on the air, I would appreciate more and more of what he represented to our lives, but also to the industry as a whole. He embodied an authentic era of sports that he never shifted from and had preserved after all these years. There he was, again celebrating the excitement and the atmosphere in everything he did. My childhood and the golden era of sports coverage were still alive through him. His was an unthinkable battle, just to be able to stand on the sideline and report again. I felt how inspiring it was, and as much as I wanted to be spending time with him, I could appreciate why he was doing it.

His attention goes entirely into living through his experiences—the bigger, the better, and the biggest moments always follow his boldness and enthusiasm for sports. He never let a press release or Twitter trend tell him what was important or what should be today's most talked-about argument. He wasn't on his phone or rushing to tweet reactions like the rest of us. In the age of tablets, iPhones, and streaming, my father was still plugged into the environment around him, blocking out everything but the fun and excitement. Just as he had taught me years ago, every game was still the most important game to him, and he emanated that mind-set once he returned to the sidelines.

It took twenty-seven years and two bone marrow transplants for me to realize that it's my dad's *perspective* that makes him one-of-a-kind, not the colorful personality and clothes that I've seen all of these years. It is what he sees, and I'm grateful every day that he fought his way back to the sidelines to remind me that sports can be an opportunity to practice enjoying every moment to its fullest.

While I searched for answers and looked for guidance, my dad, the one person I wanted to talk to most, returned to the sidelines full-time. I was beginning to realize how unimaginably difficult the past two years had been, from that first shocking phone call to a special on HBO *Real Sports*. Now April was here and I once again found myself conflicted as the playoffs approached. Was I going to get any alone time where it would be just the two of us? *I am such a different person than I was before this*, I thought. Now more than ever, I wanted that time with him. I understood myself, and the type of family we are, so much better. The playoffs arrived and there was no way he was going to be available when I needed him. Everything was back to the way it had been, except this time he had overcome two transplants to return to the sidelines and was balancing chemotherapy and blood transfusions as well.

Everywhere I went and everything I did was revolving around my dad, and I wondered if it had been that way my whole life. Every press box I went into hosted old friends of my father's who wanted to know how he was doing or to pass on their regards to him through me. Every trip to the gym or casual meeting with a friend sparked a conversation about my dad's health or when he would be back on the air. I chronicled his progress on social media for his fans to follow. I continued to listen to every interview he did in order to have the facts to give the public a glimpse into his fast-paced life and how incredible his battle was. It was tough sharing these moments from afar. No matter how happy it made me to see him back on the sidelines, there was always a part of me that wanted to be there to experience it live. But that shouldn't be surprising to a Sager. There are sacrifices that demanding jobs have on a family. I didn't understand this until I was older, but one thing our family always did was make the most out of the time we spent together. And, truth be told, there's nothing like tuning in to a game and watching him in his element. I realized that as the incredible 2016 NBA playoffs journeyed on, and watched with an appreciation I could never have imagined possible.

26

LIVING OUT LOUD

During my Northwestern years, a handful of friends and I would party in the infield of the Kentucky Derby in Louisville along with tens of thousands of others, though I was a bit more interested in the races than most. After I graduated college in 1973 and moved to Sarasota, some buddies and I decided to continue the annual pilgrimage, and so it was that Sebastian Larretta, Frank Lutostanski, Curt Malthouse, Mike Moore, Rich Rushkewicz, Tom Ryerson, Mark Sibley, Paul Tate, John Clark, and I all met in Kentucky the day before the race in 1974. My parents had close friends in Lexington, so we always had a place to crash.

On the Friday night before the Derby, our group of eager young men visited a local Lexington bar, and before long we were engrossed in conversation with a group of beautiful ladies, who happened to work as nurses in the area. Next thing I knew, it was closing time, and we all went back to the nurses' apartment complex to continue the fun. I noticed from the balcony a swimming pool in the next complex over. The pool water was an inviting shade of green, but a high metal fence separated the pool from my desire.

"I'm going swimming!" I yelled to no one in particular.

I walked down the stairs, crossed the parking lot, and climbed the fence. I jogged slowly to the diving board as my group of old and new friends cheered from the apartment balcony. When I walked to the end of the diving board, I could see just how nasty the green water actually was. I didn't care. I turned around, put my toes on the edge of the board, and did a backflip into the abyss as the fan club roared with approval.

The water was freezing, so I did not spend a lot of time in the pool celebrating my achievement. I hurriedly got out and climbed the fence again. Except that my hand slipped on one of the metal poles, and because of the way I was positioned at the time, I did the splits right on top of the fence, ripping open my groin and my inner left thigh. My friends laughed, not realizing the seriousness of my injury. Luckily, the nurses quickly came to my aid and immediately recognized that I would need a lot of stitches.

We piled into a car and raced to the emergency room, where the nurses got me in right away and a doctor inserted sixty-six stiches into my scrotum and thirty-two into my thigh. Both the nurses and my college buddies continued to drink beer while I lay in pain. The doctors suggested I spend the night in the hospital, but my friends would have none of it, and carried me off to the car.

The next morning was Derby Day and, despite my immature antics the previous night and, more practically, the injury that had almost cost me potential fatherhood, we drove from Lexington to Churchill Downs. It was too painful for me to walk, and I had bandages bulging out of my groin. The only spots left to park were a ways away from the Downs in nearby neighborhoods, and there was no way I was going to make it. One of my friends spotted a child's red wagon in the front yard of a nearby house. He gave the kid cash, and I had a mode of transportation to the infield.

There was plenty of drinking and streaking in the infield as I sat in the wagon, my shirt off and my pants still bulging with bandages. I was able to stand up but did so just at the wrong time, as police officers approached and took me into custody. My buddy Mike stood up for me, trying to explain to the officers that I was not streaking or even drinking heavily. They arrested him, too. So there we were, in glorious fashion, in the Churchill Downs jail along with forty other derelicts, most of whom were drunk beyond functioning.

Finally, after the Derby was over, the judge heard my case, and I explained the accident from the previous night.

"So you were *not* streaking?" he asked.

"No, your honor," I said. "I can't even walk."

A $220 fine later and I was free.

Reckless? Perhaps. Memorable? Absolutely. Made even more memorable by the fact that one of my buddies, Curt Malthouse, fell in love with one of the nurses, Kathy Conroy, and they married a few years later; they recently celebrated their fortieth wedding anniversary.

Taking the dare, overcoming my fears, doing the impossible—these were always part of my makeup; I thrived on high adrenaline. Hang gliding over Mexico, swimming with sharks, and jumping out of a plane for a news story. I remember being so scared free-falling over the fields of Kansas that I almost didn't pull the parachute cord. I remember touching the ground and crash-landing, thinking, *I will never do* that *again*. Of course, my cameraman, Alan Bal, wanted a different angle and made me do it again.

At the Olympic Festival in 1991 in San Antonio, my producer, Scott Cockerill, suggested that I bungee jump for a story in a parking lot set up for jumps off a very, very high crane. The instructor helped secure my harness around my hips and groin, and I swan-dived off the platform, despite having just learned that two people had already died doing the same stunt, and the jump would be shut down in a matter of days. The rush of free-falling was incredible, but the violent snap-back of the rope and harness against my body was like nothing I had ever felt before, and the remaining ups and downs as I came to a rest did not help.

It's been my MO since I was a kid—take the risks, feel the rush, live on the edge. But there is one passion in my life that slows me down. Well, sort of.

Little old Batavia did not have a golf course when I was growing up, but there were plenty of them outside of town. As my father became more successful in his career, we joined the St. Charles Country Club, where they took golf very seriously. I would swing a club with my mother when I was younger and she would constantly give me pointers: *Keep your arm straight. Stop swaying your knees. Don't grip the club so tightly.* To earn some money, I caddied a few times at St. Charles, but the arrogance of some of the young kids I was caddying for turned me off. I also worked at a public course, Old Wayne Golf Club, where I would arrive in the darkness to rake the sand traps, water the grass, and mow the greens before the first morning groups would tee off. For those of you who play golf, you know that, to protect the health of the grass, greenskeepers don't mow the greens in the same direction each day.

Our next-door neighbor in Batavia, Bill Maddox, built golf

courses all around the Midwest, including the Playboy Resort and Country Club at Lake Geneva. He hired some of us to help construct the course there in the late 1960s, and I gained an appreciation for just how critical the grain and slope of a putting green can be.

In high school, I started to play more regularly with my friends, though Batavia High School did not have a golf team. Our athletic director at the time, Bob Tober, offered to enter a few of us in the conference tournament, even though we did not have a team and had never competed in a match. So four of us—Jim Rasmussen, Robin Walch, John Clark, and I—took a shot and we finished in third place in the conference and took home a trophy without having a legitimate team and without any practice! When I got to Northwestern, I played a lot on the course near the canal, often paired with my friend and professor Gary Wodder, who had hired me to referee intramural basketball games for $25 a pop. The money came in handy—not only for expenses and beer, but to wager a bit on the golf course.

Golf stayed with me as I began my career in Sarasota, with many golf courses in South Florida, and continued in Tampa, Fort Myers, Kansas City, Atlanta, and everywhere I could find a course. I have played in PGA Tour pro-ams and in countless club and charity tournaments. I went to twenty-two straight Masters in Augusta, covered PGA tournaments, and befriended the likes of Tom Watson, Jack Nicklaus, and Phil Mickelson.

I have played more rounds of golf with Junior than with anyone else. There is drinking, wagering, and a lot of smack talk when we play. But it's a way for us to connect. After knee surgery ended my birthday tradition of running one lap for each year of my life, I turned to holes of golf. You can imagine what sixty-four holes of golf over three courses in one day can do.

I remember, when Junior was about sixteen, we played a round on Father's Day and he beat me for the first time in his life. And make no mistake, I have never believed that you should "let" your kids win in anything, so I did my best and he still beat me. I admit, I was more upset than proud. But I'm sure he sees it differently.

————

When I was a kid, Dad never let me win at anything, whether it was H-O-R-S-E or a round of golf.

I am well aware that there are two different versions of golf. There is the golf everyone else plays, and there is my dad's way of playing a round. Squeezing in a round of golf with my dad has been a father-son activity since I could first swing a club, at the age of five. The golf course has hosted some of our warmest memories and most hilarious stories. Each round awakens a rivalry abounding in pride, laughter, and getting in each other's heads. In the past several years, this has been the most efficient way to spend time with him and escape into his world of competitive fun.

After all these years of playing together, only one outing has ever ended with me celebrating victory.

Every round begins the same way. First we enter the clubhouse, no earlier than five minutes before the tee time. We make our way to the pro shop to check in and ask the most important question regarding the day's playing conditions: *Is the beer cart on the course today?* If the answer is yes, we stop at the grill and pack a cooler. If the answer is no, we stop at the grill and pack two coolers. After the cooler, or coolers, are packed with Bud Light and Bud Light only, I find my golf bag and put it on a vacant cart. Half of my clubs are probably in his bag from the last time we played—a recurring problem that I'll have to sort out later. My bag is already a random bouquet of his old clubs and ones I have accumulated over the years.

Once the bags are on, I make sure I have at least one golf ball in my bag. As long as I have one ball, I can always hunt for another one in the first woods or water hazard I come to, as Dad taught me years ago. Growing up on a golf course trained me for that.

Then it's time to floor it to the tee box. If there are any shortcuts that offer a quicker route than the cart path, I'm always prepared to take those. If there is a backup because of slow play and there are too many people on the first tee box, I'm ready to skip that hole entirely, without a verbal or nonverbal cue from him. I just keep following his cart and he'll find an opening and stop eventually.

Luckily, the course is wide-open this time. He is going to slow down and let me decide what color tee box we are playing from. He'll make it seem like my decision, but we both already know we're going to play from the blue tee box. I need the extra distance on each hole to gain any possible advantage I can. And if I suggest to him that he should play from the senior tees, I will have to face more obnoxious gloating after he beats me from the blue tees.

The rushing is temporarily done. I park the cart and try to enjoy a breath of fresh air before it's time to rush up to the tee box. Unless it is a par-3, I already know that I am taking out my driver. Using anything other than a driver will make me an easy target for insults. Even a perfect 3-wood off the tees will get me a reminder from him that I could've used a driver if I weren't a wimp. This is a lose-lose situation. I'm just going to swing as hard as I can and hopefully send a message that I came to play.

But before I think about making contact with the golf ball or how stiff I am without the slightest bit of stretching or warming up, I wait for the most important part: here come the wagers. Because there will be gambling on every hole. My dad will bet on anything: the lowest score on a hole, scoring on the front nine and the total round, closest to the pin, longest putt—you name it, he will find a way to put money on it, often with odds. Even when he plays by himself, he will often hit two balls and wager one Sager ball against the other.

I can hit the ball far and pull off a great shot every couple of holes, but my horrible short game and my average putting are no comparison to his. The better he plays, the more fun he is having. The more fun he has, the better he plays, and he is *always* having fun on the golf course. The rounds always start out competitive, but by the back nine I'm trying to regain momentum and stay focused, while he is sipping a Bud Light between birdies and pars and pushing me to pick up the pace. The second I lose my grip on the round, it is over. Before I know it, he'll be singing Queen's "We Are the Champions" on the eighteenth green, while I have to wait for him to get to his favorite verse so he can point to me while reciting, "No time for losers, 'cause we are the champions . . ."

If that's not demoralizing enough, then I have to hear the story of the first time I beat him, when I unwisely told him after the round that he would never beat me again.

"That was the best thing you could have ever told me, son," he said. "Thank you."

But not every outing is a father-son battle, and when

we are on the same team, it can be even more frenzied and competitive when our forces combine. On his fifty-first birthday, we woke up at the crack of dawn to squeeze in our new favorite tradition. On the thirty-sixth hole of the day, I got my first and only hole in one. I was fourteen years old at the time, and he bragged about it to every person we ran into the rest of the day, "This jerk just got a hole in one on *my* birthday!"

Whenever we played on the same team in tournaments over the years, it was always a party. No team was going to have more fun or take winning more seriously than ours. The more prizes and ways to gamble the better, and there is no better teammate to have in this environment than him. Every best-ball or scramble tournament we play in allows a team to drop their ball a club length from where it lands. He's taken that to a whole new level. He and his fifty-inch driver have always kept our teams out of trouble. Over time, I witnessed him go into creeks, ponds, and lakes to use this club-length rule, and all of his golfing friends could share a dozen more stories about his aquatic interpretations of the rules.

Since my dad got sick, I have played with him several times. He has worn a port in his arm and chest, bandages, layers of clothes, big hats, and even surgical masks and I have still not come close to beating him any of those times. Sure, we aren't pounding Bud Lights like we used to, and the long-drive competitions are no longer included in the list of prop bets, but these outings have been such an important source of my own strength throughout the past two years.

Each hole is like a new lease on life.

27

CAN'T STOP

On the second floor of the MD Anderson outpatient building, just above the main lobby, sits a spacious waiting room, almost the square footage of a basketball court. There are chairs and sofas and magazines, and the area is flush with sunlight from the high-paneled windows. Patients and their loved ones are everywhere, as this is where patients come to check in and wait for blood tests or to receive their chemo treatments. You can see the anguish and fatigue on the faces of many, but you can also see the hope and optimism of others.

It was early April, and I had just wrapped up the NBA regular season and returned to Houston for my eight days of chemo and a check-in with Dr. Pemmaraju. By now I had the routine down pat. I knew the registration staff, the nurses, the doctors, even some of the custodians.

As I was checking in, a woman who looked to be in her sixties approached me at the registration desk.

"Mr. Sager?" she sheepishly asked, almost embarrassed to

bother me. "I just want you to know that I am praying for you and that your fight is inspiring to many."

Now, strangers had shared similar sentiments before, but there was something so special about the words from this woman. She turned to point out her husband in a wheelchair and her grandson who had come along from Arkansas; they were seeking a miracle. They were at MD Anderson for the very first time that day, just beginning their journey.

"We are here because of you," the woman continued, and she introduced herself as Shirley Burns. "We saw that HBO story and we figured whatever hospital you were getting treatment at is where we need to be, and here we are."

After a few more minutes of encouraging words, she asked if she could pray with me.

Now, when I was younger, church was a big deal in Batavia, and though my parents were not diehards, they did make me attend religious school every Sunday. Back in those days, children who attended religious school at my church for thirteen straight Sundays were awarded a pin, and so each and every week I went, waiting till my thirteenth Sunday in a row to get that pin. When the Sunday school teacher insisted that I had attended for only twelve straight weeks, not thirteen, my mother was furious and told me, "Don't go back!" I switched denominations and started going to another church with John Clark.

I believe in God, and while I have not attended church regularly for the past two years on doctor's orders, to avoid crowds, I do believe in the power of prayer. I pray each night before I sleep, thanking God for providing me with a wonderful day, and I pray for Stacy and all five of my children. Do I believe in heaven? Sure, but I don't like talking about it.

Since my diagnosis, friends and strangers alike have sent me kind notes quoting various verses from the Bible, but based on my experience, many of the true believers struggle to explain the context and the meaning of the words. At MD Anderson, they have a minister on call, to pray with a family or to deliver last rites. Whenever he has stopped by my room to offer his company, I tell him I will gladly accept prayers, but when he offers time to play cards I tell him only if it is for money, and he quickly retreats down the hall.

Anyway, there I was, right in the middle of the hospital waiting room, sitting in a chair holding hands with a stranger as she held her husband's hand on the other side. She asked the Lord to give us both strength and to watch over us. When it was over, we hugged.

Later that day, Dr. Pemmaraju and I discussed next steps, including a still possible third stem cell transplant but from a donor other than Junior, though he acknowledged that we were a long way off from any real transplant discussion. Dr. P decided to stick with the cycle of Vidaza and Lirilumab to see where it would take us. The report was not good, but it could have been worse.

It was a full eight days in Houston, shuttling between floors and doctors and more tests. It's funny, I forget the early days of my stay at MDA, when I would notice the pamphlets on the shelf explaining the basics of AML and I would look at every fellow patient and wonder how they stacked up against my fight.

I have known NBA All-Star Dwight Howard since he was a high school legend at Southwest Atlanta Christian Academy and have followed him closely from the time he was the number-one overall pick for Orlando and spent time in Los

Angeles before coming to the Houston Rockets. (In the summer of 2016 he went home to play for the Atlanta Hawks.) Dwight was one of the first players to reach out to me after my diagnosis in 2014. It should have been no surprise that, on short notice, his foundation organized a blood drive in my honor on April 13 as the Rockets took on Sacramento and planned to recognize me at the game that night. Throughout the day, the local chapters of the Gulf Coast Regional Blood Center took donations at the Toyota Center so that perhaps, one day, they could save someone's life.

I dressed in my best red plaid jacket, red pants, and red Nikes (all FedExed to me by Stacy in Atlanta) and made my way to the arena early with some friends—Steve Henry, John Clark, John's son Jim, and Chris Landmesser. As soon as I exited the car in the parking lot, I was greeted with friendly smiles, kind words, and requests for selfies. From the guys on the street corner scalping tickets—many of whom I recognized from my visits through the years—to the security personnel to even the concession sellers, everyone offered words of encouragement and high fives. I made it a point to walk around the outside of the arena to where donors were still lined up to give blood. I met with the Blood Center staff, spoke with donors, and walked through all three donation trucks, where men and women, young and old, all colors, were lying down with needles in their arms. I even ran into Kim Presson, my physical therapist from MDA, who had been so encouraging during my exercise classes. It meant so much to me.

During a timeout in the first half of the game, the Rockets' public address announcer introduced me to the crowd as they showed me on the video board. I waved and blew kisses to the fans as they stood and cheered.

The following day, Friday, April 15, I had an afternoon reprieve from my chemo and tests at MDA, and three buddies and I went to the Wildcat Golf Club in Houston to play a round. Now, to be fair, the doctors at MDA advised against my playing golf or engaging in any type of physical activity, as my platelets and red blood cells were still low and they were concerned about bleeding. But I had always taken care of myself and was not going to waste a beautiful afternoon by sitting around in a hotel.

Dr. Pemmaraju wants all of his patients to enjoy the life that they have while battling the disease, and he has some basic rules for me to follow as I go about doing the things that I love. I must be on multiple antibiotics at all times; I must get blood work done every few days, so that doctors can proactively give me a blood transfusion if warranted; I have to wear a mask on airplanes, continually wash my hands, and otherwise avoid germs. But, boy, am I grateful for the physical condition I kept myself in leading up to my illness. I am in fairly strong shape for a sixty-five-year-old, and my body has tolerated very toxic levels of chemo over the past two years. Yes, I lost my hair at one point, but no vomiting, no nausea, no body rejection of the chemo, and no memory loss, which I'm told is very rare. Fewer than 5 percent of AML patients at my stage and level can function as fully as I have been during long stretches of my illness.

After we played eighteen holes, I felt okay. When John Clark accidently rammed his golf cart into mine, it gave me a jolt but also some contagious laughs.

"Let's keep playing," I insisted after we were done with eighteen. I was starting to feel a little tired but figured I would push through, as always. On the twenty-first hole of the day, my nose started to bleed. And bleed. I could not stop the bleeding. I thought about the doctors' concern about me bleeding, which, in my case, could actually lead to death. I put a towel around my nose and my buddies drove me back to MDA, where nurses finally stopped the bleeding and gave me yet another transfusion. And a few looks of *I told you so.*

I shrugged and smiled like the Cheshire cat.

As the NBA playoffs neared, I was even more invigorated and determined to continue working while receiving treatment. I knew that I needed to be in Houston for the monthly eight-day cycles, and it was also the optimal place for me to receive blood transfusions and platelet refills, as there was danger of infections and potential adverse reactions. On days that I would receive chemo, a transfusion, and platelets, it could take up to eight hours in the hospital.

I was hoping to be assigned to an early-round playoff series in Houston, Dallas, San Antonio, or Oklahoma City, as I could make the commute to MD Anderson to receive treatment and still never miss a game. However, Turner assigned me to the Cleveland–Detroit series, and we quickly researched hospitals where I could receive care and have my levels checked.

I felt weak during the series—perhaps the travel and the chemo were catching up with me—but I was buoyed whenever I was in the arena by everyone's kind words and hugs. When my platelet levels hit rock bottom, which is basically "walking dead," I received a blood transfusion and platelets at Sinai-Grace Hospital in Detroit, but I never missed an interview, press conference, or moment of a game.

For the Western Conference semifinals, I was assigned the San Antonio–Oklahoma City series which was great for many reasons: I knew it would be a good series, I love both cities, and I would be able to commute to Houston every day for my eight days of chemo in May. It started on May 9, when I flew in from Oklahoma City for a round of blood tests, chemo, and a consultation with Dr. Pemmaraju. Again, there was not much progress, and my blasts had inched upward a few percentage points. He wanted me to go through the current round of chemo, but we began to discuss searching for a new clinical trial. Discussions of the transplant remained on hold.

On Tuesday, May 10, I received an early-morning chemo treatment, then got into a car for a three-hour drive to San Antonio, to work the Spurs–Thunder game that night. As soon as I arrived at my hotel, the front desk relayed to me that an elderly woman had been awaiting my arrival for two days. I asked the desk clerk if she could give me more information, but alas, the elderly lady had declined to leave a message or a name.

I ran into Turner colleague Chris Webber in the lobby of the hotel, and, after exchanging pleasantries he, too, told me about an elderly lady looking for me. Just as I was about to ask if anyone had anything more than "elderly lady," a regally dressed woman rushed up to me and started to cry.

She wore brown pants with a coral blouse, a beautiful woman looking more like Betty White from *The Golden Girls* than Granny from *The Beverly Hillbillies*.

"Mr. Sager, I am Grandma Carla," she was able to get out.

It turned out that the eighty-five-year-old grandma, Carla Gomez, had flown down from Chicago just to have a chance to meet me.

"Your story is so different from anyone else's story," she shared with me through tears while grasping my hand. "You are so positive and seem to find the good in every situation." She went on tell me about her life. A lifelong sports fan who was at the game when Jackie Robinson stole home and who was once a professional ballroom dancer, Carla lives on the lake in Chicago, near Wrigley Field. A mother of five, grandmother of eight, and great-grandmother of two, Carla shared my outlook on life and radiated love and happiness.

After a few minutes of conversation, she pulled out multiple copies of the *Sports Illustrated* cover story about my fight and asked me to sign each one for her grandchildren, a photo tour of whom followed. After spending about twenty minutes together, we embraced as she offered to make a donation to help in my fight. She then headed right back to the airport to fly home.

I was stunned.

I made my way to the arena to interview Kevin Durant and then was on the sidelines for an incredible Game Five. I grabbed a few hours of sleep, and the next morning I took the first flight out to Houston for a full slate of consultations, tests, and chemo. I met with Dr. Qazilbash and although it was still a remote possibility, they were going to start the process of combing the donor registries worldwide to see if there was a match. After chemo at nine the next morning, I was in the air flying to Oklahoma City for Game Six. The very next morning, I flew back to Houston to continue the treatment. The travel was wearing on me, but the work kept me upbeat.

Though some may view my continuing to work during such a critical time in my leukemia fight as reckless or dangerous, I counter that my work is what has saved me. My work is who I am; it is the air that I breathe. I understand that some folks may question why I am not spending every day at home in Atlanta with my family when we don't know how much time I have left. I understand the question, but my answer may not be what *they* want to hear. My entire life has been devoted to playing and covering sports. I have never taken a job—nor do I continue to do my job—in search of wealth or fame. I have never had an agent in thirty-five years, and I have taken pay cuts at times in pursuit of the next challenge or opportunity. My work is who I am, for good or for bad.

There was no way that I was going to stop doing my job, unless Dr. Pemmaraju told me it could kill me—because *not* doing my job is what I knew would kill me.

28

DAY TO DAY

One afternoon during my May treatments, I felt strong enough for the half-mile walk back to the Marriott and I took my usual path, winding among the buildings of the Texas Medical Center. On this day I noticed a woman wearing a red volunteer's vest sitting on a bench outside the entrance.

"Can I talk with you for a second?" I asked as I approached her.

"Colleen Scamardi," she responded, and gestured for me to sit down next to her.

"I walk by the Children's Hospital all of the time, day and night," I said. "I see the backup of cars coming in at all hours. Just so many sick children. How do you handle it?"

She told me about the really sick children who are never allowed to leave the building and the pain and anguish she sees daily on the faces of parents. But she also shared how inspired she is by the "little faces" who battle a disease they know little about. The fight, she said, is almost passive.

"They don't think too much," she said. "They just do what they have to do . . . *to have fun*."

As she spoke, I could feel the tears forming in the corners of my eyes. We exchanged phone numbers and e-mails, and I gave her a hug and continued on my way.

I thought about who has inspired me throughout my battle. Stacy and the kids, of course, but there are others.

It was on a golf course some ten years ago that I met Major Ed Pulido. Ed was funny, compassionate, and positive in his approach to the game of golf and in his interactions with those he had never met. But it was a few years after that initial meeting, at a 2009 golf tournament at Reunion in Orlando, that I truly came to understand the power of Ed's positivity.

His father had served in the military for more than thirty years, and Ed followed in his footsteps, climbing the Army ranks to become a trusted assistant to General David Petraeus as the American military trained a new Iraqi army. On August 17, 2004, the Jeep that Ed and another soldier were riding in struck an improvised explosive device (IED) en route to a new base outside Baghdad, setting the Jeep on fire. Ed bore the brunt of the explosion, and a combat medic saved his life by pulling him from the burning vehicle. He was transported to a Baghdad hospital, then to Balad, Iraq, then on to Germany, Walter Reed Army Medical Center in Washington, and finally to a rehabilitation center in San Antonio. In late September of 2004, after doctors had done all they could to stave off a lethal infection in his left leg, they amputated it to save his life. He was hospitalized for a year and a half at one point.

The Bronze Star with Valor, the Purple Heart, and other recognitions came his way as he fought through dark times of depression and hopelessness. But soon Ed realized he had an opportunity to help others, and he has since become a leading spokesman on behalf of wounded soldiers and families who have lost a loved one. His positive energy radiates around him, which is what I felt when I first met him at a Wounded Warriors golf tournament.

"I would go back in a second," Ed shared with me before we all teed off, wanting nothing more than to have returned to Iraq to continue to serve, despite the severe costs.

When I lay in my hospital bed after my diagnosis, lamenting my lengthy hospital stay of a few months, I thought of Ed, and how he struggled for almost eighteen months in hospitals. His bravery, his relentless approach to helping others, and his true belief that every day is a gift have inspired me throughout my battle. I also thought about a little girl named Lacey.

When Lacey Holsworth was just five years old, she was diagnosed with neuroblastoma, a fatal nerve cancer, and her prognosis was grim. But doctors were discounting the power of positive thinking. In February 2012, Lacey was being treated at Sparrow Hospital in Lansing, Michigan, near the campus of Michigan State University. One day, the men's basketball team from Michigan State, led by Hall of Fame coach Tom Izzo, paid a visit to bring smiles to the children stuck in the prison of a hospital. Lacey, whose disease had left her paralyzed from the waist down, was lying on her back in the physical therapy room when the players walked in. The young basketball fan's smile grew as wide as the room as each player came in to say hello. The nurses told her that she could pick one player to stay with her as she did her painful therapy, and she selected Adreian Payne, one of the stars of the team, with a gregarious smile. Adreian stayed with her through the end of the session, and after exchanging a long hug with Lacey, he asked the nurse if he could stay in touch with his new little friend. Lacey's father, Matt, who was there for the visit, gladly passed on his information.

Over the ensuing months, Adreian and Lacey stayed in touch and became quite close. The following season, when Lacey was in remission, she went to games at the Breslin Center and cheered on the Spartans and her favorite player. I happened to be watching one of those games, and that was how I first learned of her courageous battle and her unyielding optimism, as more and more sportscasters and journalists were sharing her story and her unlikely friendship with Adreian. I soon made it a point to attend a game at Michigan State, just to be able to meet this remarkable young girl. There was something so powerful about her spirit and her smile that it truly moved me.

In November of 2013, as Lacey's disease returned with a vengeance, I did a story on her and Adreian that aired between games of the Coaches vs. Cancer doubleheader on Turner, and I saw, up close, her strength and positive attitude. When her father had the difficult conversation with his daughter about death, her response was that she was glad that she had the disease and not her younger brother, Luke, because he wouldn't understand. I stayed in touch with Matt, and by early 2014 Lacey had become a national phenomenon. She played an almost magical role as Michigan State went on a remarkable NCAA Tournament run in March, with Lacey in attendance despite her condition. On April 8, she lost her battle. She had fought like hell against her enemy and had her whole life ahead of her. Lacey was so little, with so much still to experience.

I think of Lacey often in my battle. I have had an amazing life so far and have been able to experience some wonderful

memories, so whenever my time comes, I have painted my canvas. But Lacey? She was just dipping her brush in the paint. I
fight because she fought. I will live life for both of us.

Ed and Lacey hold a special place in my heart, but I have also
been touched by the kindness of strangers who give me strength
and encouragement—like Grandma Carla. People from around
the world, some young, some old, some sports fans, some not,
some fighting their own battles, others supporting their loved
ones. Day after day, our home mailbox is filled with letters like
these:

> *My name is Spencer Bruno and I'm an aspiring sports
> broadcaster. To say you're an inspiration to not only myself,
> but every person fighting some battle every day, is an under-
> statement. I was so happy that you got to be a part of this
> year's NBA Finals. I really hope you get better soon and con-
> tinue your amazing career. It has been a privilege to watch
> you and your unique style throughout my life.*
>
> *Spencer Bruno*

He included a $5 donation.

> *Now as I am starting my own family, working my job,
> and doing all the rest of the day to day chores that we all have
> to do, at times I may think I need a rest. But then I think of
> what you must be going through and have already went
> through, and you inspire me to be better, to do more. You have
> your lovely family, still working on all the playoff NBA
> games, and all while fighting the fight of your life. It truly
> inspires me to try to do more, and just love life, and my family
> more and more each day. I really hope that I am watching you
> in your "crazy" patterned/colored suits for many more years to*

come. You are a very strong man, inspiring many, and please stay strong . . . STAY SAGER STRONG . . .

Andrew Cure

The last day of my eight-day May cycle happened to coincide with the opening game of the Western Conference finals between Golden State and Oklahoma City. I arrived at MDA well before my appointment time of 7:00 a.m., received my chemo, and raced to the airport to catch my 10:30 a.m. flight to San Francisco. Upon landing, I changed clothes and went to Oracle Arena for my pregame work and then Game One. I was so exhausted after the game that I actually shut off the ringer on my phone so I could sleep in on Tuesday morning, something I never do. After some work and some golf on Tuesday, I was back courtside for Game Two on Wednesday night, then took a red-eye flight back to Atlanta on May 18. I went right from the airport to Northside Hospital for a check-in, and, not surprisingly, I was low on blood cells and platelets. But I was home.

For two nights, I would be able to sleep in my own bed and, more important, spend time with the kids and Stacy. I also had an opportunity to replenish my wardrobe before heading to Oklahoma City for Game Three. The two games in OKC were exhilarating, but I did have a bad off day and spent much of it in an Oklahoma hospital. I figured the two bags of blood and two bags of platelets would keep me going.

The constant back-and-forth continued until the Warriors closed it out in Game Seven, a dramatic series win after trailing 3–1. The end of the series also meant the end of my NBA season. Admittedly, though, I was worn out. The travel, the transfusions, the lack of sleep had finally gotten the best of me. And besides, I expected to be back on the sidelines in October.

But then I received a call from Turner. ESPN/ABC had asked if I would like to be a part of one of the NBA Finals games as a sideline reporter. Unreal. In all my years as a broadcaster, I had never covered the Finals as a reporter. I was humbled and flattered but concerned that I not step on any toes. Of course, there was one issue: chemo.

I was scheduled to return to Houston for another eight-day cycle in June, and the only games that I could make it to would be a Game Six or Seven, if they were even played. I watched the series intently, taking notes, watching the ABC production, and otherwise preparing for an opportunity that may not happen. But it did. LeBron James carried the Cleveland Cavaliers back from a 3–1 deficit to 3–2, and I was headed to Cleveland for Game Six.

There were very few nerves on edge as I flew out to Cleveland. After all, I knew what I was doing, knew the teams and coaches, and saw this game simply as a bonus gift from both ESPN and Turner. I had worked games before with play-by-play man Mike Breen and analysts Jeff Van Gundy and Mark Jackson, so I had familiarity with the flow. The most gracious of all was sideline reporter Doris Burke, who allowed me to be a part of the broadcast and take over some of her duties during the game. I was assigned the Warriors to cover, with Doris on the Cavaliers, but Doris did tell me she wanted me to do all of the in-game coach interviews.

When it looked like Cleveland was going to win and tie the series up, I asked the ESPN producer where I should go and whom I should interview, assuming they wanted me to do a short interview with Steph Curry or Steve Kerr outside the losers' locker room.

"No, you interview LeBron on the court," Doris jumped in, insisting, and the producer agreed.

So as soon as the final horn sounded, I made my way to Le-Bron and began what was more a conversation than an interview. At the end, I had time for one more question, and I decided in that moment to just share what a fan at home was thinking.

"Congrats, a great performance. I was very pleased to be here to witness it."

"First of all, let me ask you a question," LeBron said as he put his arm around me. "How in the *hell* do you go thirty-plus years without getting a Finals game? That don't make no sense. I am happy to see you, man, much love and respect. I'm happy you were able to witness this in front of these fans. We really appreciate you."

Luckily, the director cut away to Mike Breen as my eyes began to drop tears. It was an amazing moment, yet in some ways a sad one. The NBA season was over for me. Basketball had kept me going through a rough spring as my leukemia grew in its aggressiveness, but now it was over.

For my sixty-fifth birthday in late June, Stacy, the kids, and I flew to Atlantis in the Bahamas, a family birthday tradition. We swam in the pools, fished off the islands, and soaked in the sun (although doctors warned me about too much sunlight exposure). One evening, while the kids played, Stacy sat down next to me and pulled out her cell phone. She showed me a picture of a mint condition 1968 Pontiac GTO.

"It's yours," she said excitedly. "I bought it for you from a dealer in Chicago."

It was gorgeous. A brilliant, bright red convertible, a remarkable vision of an earlier, carefree time in my life, one of the most beautifully designed and powerfully constructed muscle cars of its generation.

"I can't," I said to her, tears in my eyes. "I won't use it. The garage is filled. Let's wait until Christmas and we can buy it then."

I knew that the next several months I would be lying in hospital beds fighting for my life, and despite the extremely generous and good-hearted gift, I simply did not want the expensive present to go to waste. Besides, it would give me something to look forward to.

The prognosis from Dr. P was not good. The cycles of Lirilumab and Vidaza were not working. My blasts were up to 54 percent and growing fast. The doctors at MDA huddled and decided my best chance—perhaps my *only* chance—at survival was an intensive and toxic three-day cycle of three chemos. It would require a twenty-one-day hospital stay to monitor their effectiveness. If the new mixture worked and my blasts could be pushed down below 8 percent, doctors would immediately move to a rare third stem-cell transplant. So the prognosis was not good, but I had something that I could not miss the following week, so Dr. P and I agreed to start the cycle on July 27.

The diagnosis and plan meant that I was not going to Brazil in August to cover the Olympic Games for NBC, for what would have been my seventh straight Olympiad. I was slated to report on the USA men's basketball team and had been looking forward to it. But, to be honest, I knew deep down that with my condition worsening, Rio de Janeiro was becoming more remote, so the news that I couldn't go was not that surprising.

I had received bad news before, worse prognoses than this. Stacy and I were determined to fight through it, and I was confident that the chemo would work, that I would receive a third transplant, and that I would be around for many more years. We decided not to share the news with the family just yet.

29

ANOTHER CHANCE

I kept focus on the days that were *mine*—the twelve days before I would return to Houston for one last effort to save my life. I traveled to Batavia to play in a golf fundraiser to support the Batavia High School basketball team, and reminisced with my teammates about Coach Van. Although the town has grown since I was growing up, it still has a "Mayberry" feel even today, with the same mayor, Jeff Schielke, holding office for the past thirty-six years.

I went to Maine with Stacy, Riley, and Ryan and caught squid and lobster (and added some butter) for dinner. I returned to Batavia for a few hours to attend John Clark's daughter's wedding, as I had promised him I would back in February. By the time I made it back to Atlanta and visited Northside Hospital for blood tests, my platelet count was down to 2,000, or 2 in shorthand medical parlance. I knew that the leukemia was pushing forward.

There was one stop that I was determined to make before going to Houston, despite my condition. Stacy and I booked a room at the Ritz-Carlton resort in the Cayman Islands and we left for three nights. In the Caymans, Stacy and I went sailing on a Hobie Cat. It had been almost thirty years since I last sailed, but it came back to me quickly, and since Stacy and I were the only ones on the boat, it was a good thing that I remembered.

Being on the water with Stacy was exhilarating and refreshing and freeing. The sun beating down on my face, the spray of water misting my body, the wind moving my hair with force—I felt alive. When I turned the boat directly into the wind, I released the rudder, the sail became limp, and there was silence as the boat came to a stop. I planted a kiss on her lips and we just held hands, floating on the crystal blue water. I was living life as it was supposed to be lived, not in a hospital room. But, sadly, I knew I could not stay away forever, and we returned to Atlanta for a quick stop before flying to Houston.

Our meeting with Dr. Pemmaraju and his associates was difficult in many ways. Though he was brimming with his usual optimism and confidence, he did tell me that I had a long road ahead. Early results from my blood tests revealed my white blood count to be at very concerning levels. The leukemia was aggressive, and the cycle of three highly toxic chemos over three days was my only shot at getting into remission and then to a third transplant. Dr. P warned me that the three days would be difficult, but I paid little mind: I had been through this before. I should have listened.

Stacy was, of course, by my side every step of the way. That is, until she was prohibited. After we arrived in Houston, she had broken out in small rash splotches on her legs and arms. Stacy had suffered from a bad case of shingles when I was first diagnosed in 2014, and she was concerned that it had returned. (Later, it was determined that it was *not* shingles but rather phytophotodermatitis, a skin condition caused by sensitivity to plants or fruits.) With my immune system wiped out, Dr. Pemmaraju sent Stacy back to the hotel and, eventually, back to Atlanta. When I demanded that I at least be able to walk downstairs to say goodbye, my heart was truly breaking and I shed tears as she gingerly gave me a hug. As she walked away, it was one of the saddest moments of my life. I was going to have to get through this alone.

The next forty-eight hours, I felt more physically ill than I had ever felt during my battle. The chemo was killing all of my healthy blood cells along with the bad ones, and it was ripping my insides apart. I gained sixteen pounds over forty-eight hours because of all of the chemo and fluids, then lost thirteen pounds in a matter of hours after the chemo stopped and I was able to take Lasix to clear my organs and arteries of the excess fluid. I could barely speak, couldn't focus, and hit a wall. It was the worst that I had experienced. But I knew it was only for a few days, so I declined pain medication, believing that my mental toughness could overcome the physical.

Sure enough, within hours of ending the cycle, I started to feel better. When nurses finally detached me from my IV, I walked around the hospital floors and took laps outside in the hot Houston sun.

It would take a few weeks for the chemo to "simmer," so we would not know its level of effectiveness for days, but that didn't stop me from peppering Dr. Pemmaraju with questions about the upcoming transplant.

"Do we have the donor lined up?" *Well, there was a fourteen-for-fourteen match, but no confirmation that he or she is willing to do the transplant.*

"Well, why don't we find out if the donor is willing now?" *Relax, we are on it.*

"How many third allogeneic stem cell transplants for AML have you done this year?" *Zero.*

I was absolutely convinced that the chemo had worked and that my blasts were down to near zero. I was also convinced that I would be getting that transplant in a few weeks and that I would be back on the NBA sidelines come fall.

As you probably know about me by now, I couldn't—and wouldn't—just lie around my hospital room on the twelfth floor of MD Anderson, waiting two weeks to see if the toxic chemicals inside me were working. After the initial days of chemo, I felt remarkably fine, and there was only so much *SportsCenter* and *Gunsmoke* I could watch. So, just thirty-six hours after the last chemo treatment, I turned on my side in my bed and looked out the four-by-six-foot window with a view of the Houston skyline, the crystal blue sky, and the occasional airplane taking off or landing at nearby Hobby Airport. It was too nice a day to be a leukemia patient in dire straits.

I planned my escape. I called my good buddy and golfing partner in Houston, Steve Henry, and asked him to pull up in his pickup truck downstairs at precisely high noon. By then, I would be done receiving my platelet infusion and could get the nurses to unhook the various tubes from the port in my right arm by letting them know that I was going for a walk. I couldn't wait to enjoy the freedom of the outdoors without being tethered to IVs. My plans were dampened when a nurse informed me that I also needed a blood transfusion, but with my charm and, honestly, my resolve, we agreed that I could get the blood when "I returned from my walk."

The platelet bag finished, I jumped out of bed in my T-shirt and underwear and gingerly strode over to the closet, pulled out a vintage purple golf shirt with purple-and-pink Bermuda shorts, threw on my Nikes, and headed out the door. Yes, it was not the most inconspicuous escape wardrobe, but I figured if anyone asked, I would just tell them I wanted to feel "bright" for my walk.

On my way toward the elevators, I bumped into a few of my nurses and one of my doctors, who simply asked how I was doing. When I reached the elevator doors, I knew I was home free. (Let me be clear: I was violating hospital policies by leaving the hospital grounds.)

It was a hot day in Houston, and by hot I mean upper nineties, with a heat index well above 100. I didn't care. Didn't care that doctors did not want me in the sun; didn't care that the three intensive days of chemo were still burning inside me; didn't care that leukemia was overtaking my body. For this moment, right now, I was free. I jumped into the pickup truck and we drove the six miles to a nearby course.

As I bent over and stuck my tee in the ground in the tee box at the first hole, my biggest concern for the day was trying to avoid ripping the port that had been inserted and stitched into my arm five days earlier. It was dangling off my right arm above the elbow, but a few light practice swings convinced me I would be fine. I took a deep breath, closed my eyes for a brief second, and then *whacked* the ball. Not my best shot. As the holes progressed, my shots got progressively worse and I got progressively sick inside. The heat was overwhelming. Around the fifth hole, I knew I wouldn't make it past the front nine, but I was determined to finish. On the seventh tee, I missed my first swing, shanked the second into the marsh, and drilled another (my mulligan) into the brush. For someone who takes great pride in his golf game, this was an embarrassing disaster. My balance was off, I was nauseated, and it was hard for me to keep my eyes focused on the ball.

As I drove the golf cart toward the eighth tee, I'd had it. My stubbornness had gotten the best of me. I stopped the cart and began to vomit profusely.

"Get me inside!" I barely whispered, and, with that, we drove directly to the clubhouse as I vomited along the cart path. Once inside, cold water, a towel, and some air conditioning helped. My friends helped me to the truck and we headed back to the hospital. Even though I played horribly, got sick all over the course, and only made it through seven holes, it was well worth it.

Amazingly, I felt better within a few hours and was already thinking about my next stop that day: the Toyota Center.

The USA basketball team was preparing to leave for Brazil for the Olympics and was in Houston for one last exhibition game against the national team from Nigeria. I couldn't make it to Rio, but I was going to try my best to send them off. Of course, after the golf debacle that afternoon, and knowing that I had to receive a blood transfusion, I didn't know if the game was even a possibility. At 8:15 p.m., well after the game had started, the last drop of blood made it into my body and I was off without telling the nurses where I was headed or when I would return.

By the time I arrived at the arena, it was between the third and fourth quarters, with the Americans up by more than thirty points over a valiant but less talented Nigerian team. As I made my way to a seat near the floor, a few fans gave me a hearty cheer, and I was moved when the entire arena gave me a standing ovation after I was shown on the video board. I knew they were cheering for my battle, not for me.

After the game, to my surprise, the head of USA Basketball, Jerry Colangelo, invited me back to the team locker room. Though I'd covered the men's team at the Olympics all the way back to 1992, oddly enough I had never been in the locker room, since at the Olympics, members of the press are kept outside in a pool area and players and coaches are brought to them. After a few greetings with players and a visit with head coach Mike Krzyzewski in the coaches' locker room, Mike asked me to come with him as he addressed the team. I was honored to be allowed into the inner sanctum of sport.

After he summed up their pre-Olympics preparation and reminded them that they would be representing their country at all times, Coach Krzyzewski turned to me.

"Well, you all know Craig Sager. Craig?"

It took me a second to realize that Coach K wasn't just introducing me, but inviting me to speak to the national team. I was never a guy who gave speeches, though; I was the guy who listened to them. I was the guy who marveled at other people's talents, moments, and stories. I was the guy blessed to even witness their amazing feats. But there I stood, in front of some of the greatest basketball players and coaches in the world, their eyes looking straight into mine.

Well, thanks, guys, it is great to be here. When I first learned that you were in town, I did my best to get here, even though I didn't arrive until late in the game.

I wish you all well in Rio. I have covered every USA basketball Olympics since the Dream Team in 1992, and I had every intention to go to Rio. But with my bone marrow and leukemia blasts rising, doctors felt the timing was right for me to have a third transplant, and they found a donor match and the time is now.

I will be watching every game, and I am very proud of

you. The games won't be as easy as they were tonight. You will face hurdles. A hostile environment. Questionable offici-ating. Every team will try to foul you, especially in the back-court, to try and stop your running game. But I know you will be prepared, and with mental focus you will adjust.

My goal is to be ready for opening night in October. When I see you, I want to greet every one of you as gold medal win-ners. Good luck.

As soon as I finished my words, the team rose in unison and, one by one, led by Carmelo Anthony, came over and gave me a hug, many offering their prayers and support. It was one of the proudest moments of my life and capped a day in Hous-ton that I will never forget.

The next day was even better, as doctors informed me that the anonymous donor had agreed to the procedure and the third transplant was on for August 31. One last chance.

30

Lessons from My Father

What I *learned* from my father, and what my father
taught me growing up, most people would assume to be
one and the same. What I *learned* from him continues to
evolve, years after our nostalgic escapades. What I was
taught by my father was simple: (1) how to make the most
of the one life we are given, and (2) to always find the fun.
Don't get me wrong: my father is not naive with this
twofold advice. He is well aware that making the most
out of life while still managing to find the fun cannot be
achieved by simply wishing it to be so. My father's unparalleled work ethic, in combination with his unwillingness
to accept no for an answer, is the most valuable quality
I've learned, and one that I have strived to embody my
entire life.

Even things my dad didn't teach me how to do, I still
picked up, as a result of our special Sager bond. Any time
I'd get discouraged after losing, he would rub it in my face
a little more and then remind me that I would be able to

beat him at everything one day and to keep practicing. This father-son rivalry shaped me.

He was my teacher, and I wanted to make sure I made the most out of what I had. I could learn from his successes and find the things that he wasn't doing that I could do. I began to search for any possible advantage I could use to become better than him when I was older. I developed the mind-set that if he was this good without doing these particular things, then how good could I be if I *did* do them?

He is a good athlete, but they didn't really lift weights when he was growing up, I'd think to myself. That motivated me to start lifting weights. *When he was growing up, they didn't have nutrition plans.* I started studying nutrition and used my diet to gain another possible edge.

My entire family was always challenging one another to be better. My dad just happened to be my toughest challenge and biggest motivation wrapped into one. I felt the pressure to follow in his footsteps every day of my life. That stress was suffocating until a challenge came my way. Then it became my fuel and my biggest source of strength.

These lessons and beliefs changed the moment my dad got sick. I thought I had to become my own teacher, even though I hadn't yet found the version of myself I'd be teaching. Unlike my dad, who was always a Pollyanna and unapologetically himself, I was an unintentional pessimist with a full assortment of emotions. I had worn every emotion over the years and let them all guide me at some point.

I started to look back at all the things I had learned from my dad that could help me get through the frightening road ahead. I began to realize that what I learned from him and what he taught me *were* one and the same. All those years, he was unwittingly teaching me how to teach myself. The unpredictable lifestyle, the work ethic, and his unshakable outlook on life weren't just the fundamental skills I thought they were when I was growing up. These were the invaluable qualities that he passed on to me that could prepare me for the curve balls life would throw. The ability to adapt and to embrace change was already a part of me.

Two years into his battle with AML, his influence continues to structure my attitude toward life. When a difficult situation comes about, I no longer ask myself, *How will this change my life?* He taught me that it will change my life however I choose to let it. The goals that I used to let control me can now guide me. By placing more meaning in the "little things" and the present moment, rather than the goal itself, it has been more rewarding and effective in improving me as a person.

I doubt I will ever be able to be as positive as my father, but I have never met anyone else able to replicate his positivity, so I can't really blame myself. What I can do and what anyone can do is bring the same passion into each day that he does. I no longer fear my emotions or let them hold me back, because he showed me that being positive is always possible. No matter how hard life may seem to me at times, I know that my dad would still be able to find the fun somewhere. And that promise of hope that he gave me will always be my strongest suit.

31

NEVER, EVER GIVE UP

I first met Jim Valvano in the 1980s, when he was a frequent guest on our CNN *College Coaches Corner* show based in Atlanta, as he was always in the area recruiting the next North Carolina State basketball phenom. Jim was gregarious, compassionate, and hysterical on the air and off. Born in Queens and raised on Long Island, he had that "it" gene, turning a roomful of strangers into friends within minutes. Most of America knew Jim as the crazy coach who led N.C. State to the 1983 national championship and then ran around the court after the game-winning shot, searching for someone to hug. When he stepped away from coaching in 1990, he transitioned into the world of television, and Turner hired him to be a color analyst at the 1991 Pan Am Games in Cuba. He was spectacular on the air. When we weren't courtside for a game, we would go out as a group in Havana, and Jim was just as kind with the Cuban youth as he was with his colleagues, often stopping and shooting hoops with them on makeshift baskets on the sidewalks of the city.

In June 1992, Jim was diagnosed with adenocarcinoma, a deadly form of bone cancer. When I first heard the news, I got a pit in my stomach. But he attacked life like I did, living every moment, cherishing every breath, looking for the positives in people and in events.

Jim's cancer progressed rapidly, but he never lost his iconic jet-black hair from the chemo, nor were there many *visible* signs of his pain and disease. In February 1993, he took the stage at the ESPY Awards to receive the Arthur Ashe Courage Award. Many of us then, and since, have watched his remarkable speech in awe. Some excerpts:

> *When people say to me, "How do you get through life or each day?" it's the same thing. To me, there are three things we all should do every day. We should do this every day of our lives. Number one is laugh. You should laugh every day. Number two is think. You should spend some time in thought. Number three is you should have your emotions moved to tears—could be happiness or joy. But think about it. If you laugh, you think, and you cry, that's a full day. That's a heck of a day. You do that seven days a week, you're going to have something special. . . .*
>
> *I just got one last thing. I urge all of you—all of you—to enjoy your life, the precious moments you have. To spend each day with some laughter and some thought, to get your emotions going. To be enthusiastic every day. As Ralph Waldo Emerson said, "Nothing great could be accomplished without enthusiasm"—to keep your dreams alive in spite of problems, whatever you have. The ability to be able to work hard for your dreams to come true, to become a reality. . . .*
>
> *I know, I gotta go, I gotta go, and I got one last thing: I said it before, and I want to say it again. Cancer can take*

away all my physical abilities. It cannot touch my mind, it cannot touch my heart, and it cannot touch my soul. And those three things are going to carry on forever. I thank you, and God bless you all.

Twenty years later, I think of my friend and his words almost every day. *Don't give up, don't ever give up.* I can't give up; I won't. I downloaded Jim's ESPY speech onto my phone and pull it out when I need a pick-me-up. And I *would* need it, many times over.

Back in May, when I was in Houston, my cell phone rang while I was hooked up to a chemo IV, and Stacy's number appeared on my caller ID.

"Hello, Luv."

"Craig, my name is Maura Mandt, and I am on the line with your wife, Stacy," said an unfamiliar voice. "I am the executive producer of the ESPY Awards, and we would like to honor you this year with the Jimmy V Perseverance Award."

I can't recall my first response exactly, but I am sure it was silence followed by something like "No way." The thought that I would be honored in the same manner that Jim Valvano and so many other courageous and brave men and women have been recognized was almost too preposterous to believe.

After accepting the reality of the invitation, I immediately began thinking of two things: What would I wear and what would I say? This would be a night above all other nights. A chance to stand onstage in Los Angeles, with millions watching at home, and encourage others to never give up and to fight, and to also raise awareness for cancer research. It was a platform that I could not let go to waste.

I settled on a suit from Rex Fabrics in Miami. It was a cheetah-patterned black-white-and-yellow suit jacket, to be worn with a yellow shirt and brown pants. Fratelli made a tie to match that was designed at A. Taghi in Houston. My friends at Nike made leopard-print sneakers in matching colors, with the words MR. FANCY and SUITS on the tongues. The ensemble was set and, truly, was like none other that I had ever worn. Now my attention turned to my speech.

I wanted to inspire, I wanted to let people know that no matter what they were going through, if they simply had the right attitude, they could make it. I watched Jimmy V's speech again and again for inspiration. Hope is not a strategy, of course, but it is a foundation for taking challenges head-on. As I thought about the best way to get my message across, I thought of a train set in the Children's Hospital in Houston. I don't know why it came to mind, but there was just something about the display, so I crafted a speech around the trains.

As a young boy, I had the usual hobbies—sports, baseball cards, model airplanes, and trains. But I always had a distinct fascination with trains. The freight trains would run on the CBQ line from Chicago to Quincy or the northwestern line from Aurora to Elgin and come through Batavia three to four times a day, slowing to a walk as they passed by—and occasionally stopping at the metal factory or the lumberyard. The trains had first become a staple in Batavia after the devastating Chicago Fire of 1871, when limestone was dug from a quarry just outside of town and transported to Chicago to help rebuild the city. Despite the slow speed of each train, you could hear the roar of the engine and feel the rumble of the cars from the sandlots down Batavia Avenue to the classrooms of the elementary schools. For a tiny, nondescript Midwestern town like Batavia,

Illinois, in the 1950s and '60s, the trains were a welcome diversion from the routine of small-town life.

When I was a young lad, my best friends and I, including John Clark, Tom Cornwell, and Greg Issel, used the trains as a diversion—as entertainment on slow summer days or late-spring afternoons. There were days when we brought spare change we dug up from the sofas in our homes and placed the coins on the metal rails as the trains approached, hoping that the sheer force and weight of the rigs would provide us with a perfectly smooshed nickel. It was a science, really: more times than not, the rumbling of the cars would knock the coin off before impact or the weight would simply crush it into an unrecognizable piece of scrap. But on one occasion, if we placed it *just right*, and with a little luck from the train gods, we would have ourselves a souvenir.

But the trains provided more than just metal. We would often jump into an open cargo car as we jogged alongside it, hopping for a ride to the nearby quarry to swim or for the brief two-mile lift to nearby Geneva. Or we would race alongside the freight as it sped up leaving town, the tracks winding parallel to the Fox River. When the tracks were empty, which was most of the day, we would challenge one another to see who could maintain their balance the farthest on the rails, or simply follow the still tracks out of town, one way or the other.

Like most boys, I had a model train set up in my bedroom upstairs, resting on a little-used Ping-Pong table. My first set was mainly Lionel cars, but as the Cold War became fashionable, many of my cars were replaced by blue-and-white military replicas, complete with rockets invariably aimed at the Soviet Union that could be "launched" by hand, and a helicopter that "took off" with the push of a button. Many Christmases, Mom and Dad would deliver me yet another car, and the oval track that was attached to plywood kept growing in size. I could watch the train go round and round on the short loop, time after time, as if expecting something to change. But it never did.

Almost fifty years later in Houston, I found myself once again mesmerized by a train, this time at the Children's Hospital. At night, on my walks back to the hotel after a long day of treatment, I would step inside and stand in the silence. Those moments would become the storyline of my ESPY speech.

All of my children; Stacy; my sister, Candy; my mother-in-law; and one of Stacy's brothers and his family all flew to Los Angeles on Monday evening, July 11, courtesy of a private jet provided by ESPN. It was such a joy to see the younger kids' wide-eyed smiles as they boarded the plane. As soon as we landed, I was driven to the Microsoft Theater in downtown Los Angeles to rehearse my speech. Producers previewed for me the six-minute video feature that ESPN had been working on for months with Ron Howard, and it brought me to tears. To see my son Craig cry on camera, to see Stacy so bravely talk about our fight, was overwhelming. But I collected my emotions and rehearsed the speech, trying to not rely on the teleprompters.

The following day, I participated in the ESPY Celebrity Golf Classic to raise money for cancer, and that evening we attended a pre-party at a hip club in Hollywood along with Dwyane Wade and other stars. Honestly, I was tired. It had been a long few days. At 10:40 p.m., we left to return to the hotel, where I stayed up to rehearse my speech.

Wednesday afternoon was in the nineties in Southern California, and it was hot as we stepped out of our cars onto the red carpet leading into the theater. As we walked through the gauntlet of reporters, I ran into my friends Ernie Johnson and Charles Barkley and NBA commissioner Adam Silver. It must have taken more than an hour for us to get through the red carpet and to finally take our seats.

As the show got started, I grabbed Stacy's hand. I knew that my segment was later in the show, and during an early commercial break, I took the opportunity to get up from my seat and walk out of the exit to a concourse. I found an exterior door to a parking lot and asked the security guard to allow me outside for a few minutes. So there I was, in the middle of the ESPY show, standing alone in a parking lot, rehearsing my speech three times, complete with hand gestures and pauses. I was determined to not use the teleprompter and to keep eye contact with the audience.

When I returned to my seat, NBA MVP Steph Curry took the stage to present the Arthur Ashe Courage Award to the family of Zaevion Dobson, a Knoxville, Tennessee, fifteen-year-old who was shot and killed in December 2015 while saving the lives of two of his friends. His mother, Zenobia, and brothers, Zack and Markastin, made an emotional walk up to the stage while superstar athletes cried in their seats. As Zenobia gave a brilliant, emotional, and impassioned plea to end gun violence, I cried. I cried for Zaevion, I cried for his family, I cried for children everywhere, including my own.

A week before the ESPYs, I had received a call from a producer who told me I would be presented with the ESPY Award by Vice President Joe Biden. Vice President Biden had recently launched the "Cancer Moonshot," a campaign to finally eradicate cancer across humanity. He had lost his eldest son, Beau, in May 2015 to brain cancer, and the ESPYs were giving him a platform to raise awareness. A few months earlier, at the Final Four in Houston, the vice president had pulled me aside to express his support in my battle and to remind me that he was working on the Moonshot.

He came to the stage at the ESPYs with Beau on his mind.

> *Like Jimmy V, my son Beau never let cancer touch his heart, or his soul. Till the end, my Beau worried about his family more than himself. He lived his entire life by my father's code, which was: Never explain, never complain, just get up. Just as Jimmy V's life inspired the creation of the Jimmy V Foundation for Cancer Research, Beau Biden's life and concern for others inspired the Cancer Moonshot, the national effort President Obama asked me to lead to finally end cancer as we know it. Ladies and gentlemen, it won't be easy, but it is possible, because we are America, and like Jimmy, like Beau, and like Craig Sager and countless others, we never, ever give up. Tonight we honor Craig, a man of courage and loyalty, with a hell of a team behind him, like Jimmy and like Beau had: fans, coaches, colleagues, players, the country. But most importantly, Stacy, Kacy, Krista, Riley, Ryan, and Craig Junior. His home team, his family. Craig knows that every day, every hour, every moment matters, and by his conduct he teaches us about how to live with perseverance and passion. Fearless, hopeful, together.*

As the video feature played for those in the theater and around the country, detailing my fight and my unwillingness to give in, Stacy and I held hands. I was worried about breaking down during my speech, overcome with emotion and the moment. But that thought passed: I wanted the ball in my hands with the shot clock winding down.

"Give me strength," I asked her.

"You will do great," she told me.

When the video piece ended, the audience rose to its feet in applause, and I made my way up the steps to the stage, where I gave the vice president a hug and acknowledged the kind applause from the audience.

Walking up onto the stage was surreal and uncomfortable in a way. Here I was, the guy who has spent his life asking questions of the biggest names in sports and hanging on their every word, about to speak *to* them. I spotted Kareem Abdul-Jabbar and LeBron James, Peyton Manning and Kobe Bryant, all looking at me, staring in silence.

Well, first of all, thank you, Mr. Vice President, for the kind words and the struggles you had with your son Beau. Your amazing fight, your determination, dedication, putting your whole career, your whole life, forward to finding a cure for cancer. I am confident in you that one day soon, we will wipe out cancer.

I'd like to thank ESPN for this honor. Jimmy V's inspirational message is on my phone, a constant source of encouragement and inspiration, and it is always at my bedside in the hospital and I can listen to it anytime I want. So my thoughts are with the Valvano family, because this honor means a great deal to me, so thank you very much.

I'd also like to thank my two families that are here. You saw their pictures. First, my beloved bride, Stacy. She is my heaven on earth. In the darkest of moments, tears running down her cheeks, we embraced and we prayed. "Please, don't leave me," she pleaded. "We can fight this together." There is no fear in love, and your love is my strength. My children, Kacy, Craig, Krista, Riley, Ryan, my sister, Candy, Stacy's mother, Mary Jo: my battle has been your battle.

I would also like to thank my Turner Sports family.

Many of them are here tonight: David Levy, Lenny Daniels, Craig Barry, Scooter Vertino, Matt Hong, Nate Smeltz. Your love and support since my first diagnosis has been incredible, and your willingness to adapt to let me keep doing what I love is something I will never forget.

And the truth is that the Turner family is just part of a bigger family—all of you, the sports family. Sports are who I am in my soul, they have guided my life, and I have had the good fortune to witness all of your amazing feats. And I am confident that I will continue to watch those amazing feats.

I have spent most of the past year and a half at the most impactful cancer hospital in the world, MD Anderson in Houston. And many nights I don't get out of the hospital until well after midnight, and I always take the same walking path back to the hotel. The sidewalks wind through a maze of buildings, including the Texas Children's Hospital. Many nights, I will stop, pause, and I will go inside. And a few feet inside the hallway is this large model train display, covered by glass. There are seven buttons on the outside; they activate the trains, the circus, the toys, and the trolley. And many nights, alone, in the stillness and solitude of the hospital, I push those buttons, and I watch the trains as they disappear through the tunnels and emerge, full steam, on the other side. I watch the trains as they pass by the town square, the dinosaur canyon, the pirates' cove, Santa Land, and the ice skating rink. And I sit there, and I watch, and I listen. I listen to the sounds of the circus, of the kids laughing, and of the train chugging along.

Now, I don't know why I am so drawn to this train set. Perhaps it's my life coming full circle. Maybe it's just the kid inside all of us. Or perhaps it's a few minutes of my life that leukemia cannot take from me.

The train actually takes two minutes and twenty seconds to make a full loop. But what is time, really? When you are diagnosed with a terminal disease like cancer, leukemia, your perception of time changes. When doctors tell you you have three weeks to live, do you try to live a lifetime of moments in three weeks, or do you say, "The hell with three weeks"? When doctors tell you that your only hope of survival is fourteen straight days of intense chemotherapy, twenty-four hours a day, do you sit there and count down the 336 hours, or do you see each day as a blessing? Time is something that cannot be bought, it cannot be wagered with God, and it is not in endless supply. Time is simply how you live your life.

I am not an expert on time or on cancer or on life itself. I am a kid from the small Illinois town of Batavia who grew up on the Chicago Cubs and made sports his life's work—although there has never been a day where it actually seemed like work. I have run with the bulls in Pamplona; I have raced with Mario Andretti in Indianapolis; I have climbed the Great Wall of China; I have jumped out of airplanes over Kansas; I have wrestled gators in Florida; I have sailed the ocean with Ted Turner; I have swam with the sharks in the Caribbean . . . and I have interviewed Gregg Popovich—mid-game, Spurs down seven.

If I have learned anything through all of this, it's that each and every day is a canvas waiting to be painted. An opportunity for love, for fun, for living, for learning.

To those of you out there who are suffering from cancer, facing adversity: I want you to know that your will to live and to fight cancer can make all the difference in the world. The way you think influences the way you feel, and the way you feel determines how you act. And to everybody out there: we are making progress—incredible progress, as the vice pres-

ident said—the Moonshot program—we are going to find a cure for cancer. But we need your help: we must continue to donate, we must continue to fight, and we must continue to do this together.

I am grateful to my parents, Coral and Al. They raised me with a positive outlook on life. I always see the glass half full. I see the beauty in others, and I see the hope for tomorrow. If we don't have hope and faith, we have nothing.

Whatever I might have imagined a terminal diagnosis would do to my spirit, it summoned quite the opposite—the greatest appreciation for life itself. So I will never give up, and I will never give in. I will continue to keep fighting, sucking the marrow out of life as life sucks the marrow out of me. I will live my life full of love and full of fun. It's the only way I know how.

Thank you and goodnight.

EPILOGUE

After spending so much time at MD Anderson, my view on hospitals has changed. Instead of being a place of despair and last resorts, it is a place of hope, of innovation, and of possibilities. Patients know they are receiving the best treatment in the world, and their loved ones know that they are being taken care of. Patients see the results of the lifesaving clinical trials, and the doctors and nurses foster optimism. When I walk the halls of the hospitals in Atlanta and Houston and I see so many others in a great deal of pain and suffering, I am grateful that I have the resources and support to have access to the best doctors and clinical trials in the world.

I am in uncharted territory with my treatment. I am told that very few patients have two bone marrow transplants, let alone three. As of this writing, I am now two weeks post–third transplant, and I am confident I'll make it back. I am also told that even fewer patients could have survived fourteen straight days of twenty-four-hour-a-day chemotherapy. And that yet even fewer have been given a prognosis of "three to four weeks" or "two weeks" and come out on the other side. And I'm proud to be that kind of statistic. As I write this, I have lost a great deal of my hair and my weight, but not my spirit.

I don't know where my journey will take me next, but I do know that each and every day is a canvas, just waiting to be painted.

With the outpouring of love and wishes from so many and the impact my fight seems to have on others, I have wondered during the past few years if all of this is about serving a greater purpose. There must be some reason that I have survived three stem cell transplants and enough chemo to power New York City, and have overcome remarkable odds to still be living today. It can't just be that God wants me to keep enjoying my life. Perhaps God is keeping me around to give hope to others, to spread awareness, to keep life upbeat?

I truly believe that miracles do happen and that I will be a medical miracle. A positive attitude actually can have an impact on my health—something that Dr. Pemmaraju agrees with, by the way. I also believe that you can't fight this battle alone, that you need to surround yourself with loving family and friends who will remain as positive as you.

I have very few regrets. In fact, as I write that, I realize: I don't think I have any—though I do want to travel to one more place. When my mother died a few years ago, she was cremated, and she said she wanted her ashes spread in the wilderness of Africa. First work and then the leukemia prevented me from honoring her wishes, but I will. For now, Mom rests in my sister's house.

I have traveled the world, been to the greatest sporting events, run the Olympic marathon course in Athens, Greece (with a few beer stops along the way), thrown out the first pitch at Wrigley Field, had five amazing kids, been in love, and met so many wonderful people. Strange as it may sound, the disease has given me the opportunity to meet even more folks and continue the cycle of positivity that has been so instrumental in getting me to where I am, which I can only describe as a place of sincere gratitude.

I was asked in an interview once what my philosophy on life was, and the answer is really rather simple: enjoy it. None of us knows when our ride is going to end. Mine may have passed by the time you read this page, or I may live another thirty years—you know which option I believe will happen!

As I lie in a hospital bed in Houston, my mind takes me to the milestones yet to be reached that I want to bear witness to: the dramatic end-of-game shots that make mortals into immortals; the crowning of new champions; the simplicity and rhythm of a midsummer night's baseball game with no bearing on the standings. I want to see it all.

And I am confident that I will. I believe with all of my heart that I will be on the NBA sidelines again and that I will grow old with Stacy and watch my children enjoy life's experiences as I did. And I am not giving back my ESPY.

Oh, and by the way—my first pitch at the Chicago Cubs game in June? High and wide, but made it the sixty feet, six inches.

ACKNOWLEDGMENTS

One thing that I hope you took away from the preceding pages is an understanding of my undying love and admiration for Stacy. She came into my life and simply changed it—and me—forever. She has been a wife, a mother, a best friend, a caretaker, an organizer, and, simply, an angel. Every day with her is a blessing, and she is the reason why I am still enjoying life.

All five of my children—Kacy, Craig, Krista, Riley, and Ryan—have made my life such a joy. I pray for their futures, and I know that they will find happiness and success on the road that lies ahead. If I could pass on any advice to my children, it would be this:

You have nothing without hope. Always believe that better days lie ahead and that the next day, the next golf shot, the next exam, the next run, will be better.

Rules are for people without brains. Use common sense, to experience the thrills that life affords us and to push the boundaries of what you think you can do. If you have smarts, you don't need rules.

Create your own luck. As I did with Hank Aaron and Seattle Slew and during many of my stops in my career, work hard and put yourself in a position to be lucky. It works.

Don't take no for an answer. Be persistent, find ways to a yes, and, if needed, use a boat.

Turn a negative into a positive. Throughout my life, I have taken challenges and obstacles and turned them in my favor—not because I am who I am, but because I take the right attitude.

Be who you are. If I worried about what others thought of my appetite for fun, of my bright wardrobe, of choices that I have made, then I would not be who I am today. Love yourself, and remember, being different can be a good thing.

Get busy living or get busy dying. There will be plenty of time to rest when you are gone. Experience as much as you can during your life, as you won't want to miss a thing.

Over the past few years, Stacy could not have been by my side without the love and support of her mother, Mary Jo Strebel, who has stepped up in emergencies and over long periods of time to care for Riley and Ryan and to keep things running smoothly in Atlanta. She is a truly amazing woman, and I am forever indebted to her.

My sister, Candy Menzemer, has been with me the longest, and though she may not have liked me much when I was a younger pain, she has never been anything less than a wonderful big sister.

My parents did not give me a brother, but Batavia did, and John "Hondo" Clark has been my best friend since I was a toddler. Hondo and his wife, Karol, have been there in good times and bad, and outside of Stacy, there is no one I trust more in this world than him. I couldn't imagine a better brother. Paula Issel and Jimmy Roberts, and all of the Batavia gang continue to be a part of my life, and I am grateful for their love and support, as well as Terry Thimlar, Margaret Sirianni, and my friends in Florida.

There are so many colleagues and friends from over the years to thank, but let me acknowledge a few. David Levy and the staff at Turner have been my family for more than three decades, and never more so than in the past two and a half years, with their unwavering support. You have provided me with a lifetime of memories. To Ernie Johnson, Charles Barkley, Kenny Smith, and Shaquille O'Neal, producer Tim Kiely, Tara August and Olivia Scarlett, who are tremendous friends and colleagues, thank you. I am also grateful to the teams at ABC/ESPN, CBS, and NBC for the opportunities of a lifetime.

The members of the NBA basketball community have brought me to tears with their generous love and support the past few years. I want to thank Commissioner Adam Silver and the league office, Bob Delaney and the officials, the coaches, the team PR directors, the colorful fans, and, of course, the players. In particular, thank you to Steph Curry, Kevin Garnett, Dwight Howard, LeBron James, and Dwyane Wade for supporting me and my battle. It is an honor to witness your passion and skills.

I also want to thank Jerry Colangelo and the USA men's basketball team for their kindness and compassion. There was no place in the world that I wanted to be more than Rio de Janeiro this summer, and I could not have been more proud to see them take home the gold again. My gratitude to Mike Krzyzewski, Jim Boeheim, Tom Thibodeau, and Monty Williams, and the players: Carmelo Anthony, Harrison Barnes, Jimmy Butler, DeMarcus Cousins, DeMar DeRozan, Kevin Durant, Paul George, Draymond Green, Kyrie Irving, DeAndre Jordan, Kyle Lowry, and Klay Thompson. Thank you.

How do you thank those who have truly saved your life,

time and time again? A mere "thank you" seems unreasonable and inadequate. I am grateful to the wonderful doctors and nurses at Northside Hospital in Atlanta, particularly Dr. Kent Holland, who got me past my first year of the battle and my first transplant. I became close with Anslee Ward, an oncology nurse, who not only nurtured my daily care but did it with a pleasant confidence and assuring approach, even feigning interest in my habitual viewing of long-ago television shows, as well as Janet Benn, who was there for me when I needed a smile or just a distraction. And, yes, Raphella Stovall, who makes giving blood in the mornings easy and fun!

Once I arrived at MD Anderson, I was blown away by the skill and compassion of the medical staff, and it starts at the top, with Dr. Ronald DePinho, who has become a good friend and counselor. No words can adequately describe what Dr. Naveen Pemmaraju has meant to Stacy and me. He is not only my savior but a true partner, and I only wish that everyone battling cancer could have Dr. P at his or her side. Dr. Qazilbash saw me through two stem cell transplants and a lot of chemotherapy and has saved or prolonged many lives, including mine. The nurses and support staff have been great, and I found one nurse in particular, Mary Elliott, at MD Anderson, who has an unparalleled touch with bone marrow extraction and massage that is soothing and comforting. Don't get me wrong: it still hurts like hell, but at least Mary makes it somewhat bearable.

Hank and Kelley Cook, Sam and Susan Blair, Mike Joehl, Bob Beardslee, and all of those who have been instrumental in the SagerStrong Foundation, your work has meant so much to me, but, more important, to those who will come long after. My thanks as well to the Chicago Cubs and ESPN for providing me with the thrill of a lifetime, and to Mark Thomashow and Lynn Merritt at Nike for their continued love and support.

I had no idea what would go into writing a book, and, honestly, I was hesitant at the start, but it became a fun passion and a much-needed distraction. My sincere gratitude to my son Craig, whose tremendous writing is evident in these pages and who was willing to share the perspective of a family member. Of course, I can never thank Craig enough for extending my life twice. I love you.

The saying "better late than never" certainly applies to Brian Curtis coming into my life. Not only is he a talented author, but he quickly became a friend and confidant to Stacy and me. I hope that we can continue the jokes for a long time to come.

My thanks to Bob Miller and the incredible team at Flatiron Books for believing in me and my story. Jasmine Faustino, Steven Boriack, Marlena Bittner, Liz Keenan, Molly Fonseca, Ben Tomek, David Lott, Emily Walters, Steven Seighman, and Vincent Stanley made this process so easy and were great partners in pushing to get this book into the hands of readers. Thanks as well to our agent, Gary Morris, at the David Black Agency, for moving this project along.

Finally, thank you to all of you around the world who have inspired me with your kind words, your letters, and your stories. I am amazed at the kindness and hope in this world; the future is bright for my children.